THE FIGHT FOR FREEDOM

A Memoir of My Years in the
Civil Rights Movement

JOHN REYNOLDS

authorHOUSE®

AuthorHouse™
1663 Liberty Drive
Bloomington, IN 47403
www.authorhouse.com
Phone: 1-800-839-8640

Published by AuthorHouse 5/29/2012

ISBN: 978-1-4772-1012-3 (eBook)
ISBN: 978-1-4772-1013-0 (hardcover)
ISBN: 978-1-4772-1014-7 (softcover)
ISBN: 978-1-4969-3229-7 (audio)

Library of Congress Control Number: 2012909011

Print information available on the last page.

To my beloved wife Gloria,
whose love and patience has enriched my life

To my daughters, Martina and Danielle,
who I hope will stand up for what is right in their generation

To Leon Gutherz, the man who changed my life forever

To the brave freedom fighters that I fought alongside

Contents

Acknowledgments ix

Introduction xi

Life on a Plantation 1

Change Comes to My Hometown 11

A New Life 33

The King/Abernathy Partnership 39

Getting Ready for the Fight 45

Selma 51

Greene County, Alabama 63

The Meredith March 69

Chicago with Dr. King 75

A Sabbatical to New York 83

Birmingham 89

Greensboro, Alabama 95

Dr. King's Vision of a Poor People's Campaign 115

The Death of Dr. King 121

The Poor People's Campaign 131

Resurrection City 137

The Holy City 149

The Native Americans of Ridgeville 163

Providence 179

Life after SCLC 187

Settling Down 193

Some Thoughts about SCLC 199

Not in Vain 203

Acknowledgments

First of all, I need to acknowledge and thank all of those freedom fighters that I worked with in SCLC–Albert Turner, James Orange, Thomas Gilmore, Tom Offenburger, Terrie Randolph, and many, many others. I also want to thank local leaders in the various communities where I worked–Johnnie Mae Warren of Troy, Alabama; Theresa Burroughs of Greensboro, Alabama; Michael VanLeestan of Providence, Rhode Island; and Victoria DeLee of Ridgeville, South Carolina. I hope I have honored them by telling their stories as well as my own.

I want to thank my mother, Mattie Lue Reynolds, for her love and support. Although she was afraid for me, I thank her for not trying to stop her teenage son from doing what he knew he must do. I need to acknowledge my late father, Henry Reynolds. It may have taken him longer to accept the path I had chosen, but when his support came, it came with love and pride. I thank my stepmother, Patsy Reynolds, whose faith and love for me never wavered, even during the most difficult times.

I want to express my gratitude to two people who were at the very start of my journey in 1965: Danny Thompson, a young white man I saw talking to an elderly black woman with such respect that I knew he must be a civil rights worker. Danny brought me to his project leader, Leon Gutherz, a man who has been in my life from that day to this and whom I have counted upon for so many things that I can never thank him enough. Although she is gone from us now, I also need to acknowledge the importance of Septima Clark in my journey.

This book would not have happened without the support and hard work of my wife, Gloria, for she was there when it was only a dream. She has been there from the very first word that was put on the page right to the very end–typing and proofreading the manuscript as it grew. Without her, it would still be a dream. Many others were instrumental in making this book a reality as well:

My editor, Ellie Maas Davis, who believed in this project and continually challenged me.

Helene Gutherz, who encouraged me over the years and shared the photographs she had taken in 1969 of the Poor People's Campaign in Washington, DC, and the Ridgeville school in South Carolina. Most of my photographs from those years were lost in a house fire many years ago, so her pictures helped jog my memory of these events. Helene's son, Steve Gutherz, shared with me a daily journal, created by Frechettia Ford, of the activities that took place in Troy, Alabama, during the first few weeks after I joined the civil rights workers in 1965. This information was immensely helpful in getting started on this book.

Nena Jackson, whom I met soon after we moved to South Carolina, was working on her own book as I began mine, and she was extremely generous in sharing her experiences. When I reached the stage of looking for an editor and a publisher, McKendree "Mike" Long III, a published author, was especially helpful. Reverend Lynne Holden, a colleague from Rhode Island, had also recently written a book. Encouragement and advice from these three author friends was extremely helpful in completing my manuscript and getting it published.

My next-door neighbor, Philip Bach, who graciously and tirelessly shared his impressive photographic skills. He helped to restore older photographs, as well as properly prepare and organize photographs for this publication.

My closest friend, Reggie Jones, who encouraged me throughout this process.

Aimee Reff at AuthorHouse, who kept me motivated during the early months of this process. Thanks to the rest of the AuthorHouse team as well.

Introduction

I was blessed to have been able to participate in one of the most tumultuous periods in our country's history and to work alongside such giants as Martin Luther King, Jr. and Ralph David Abernathy. I moved from awe and respect for these two men when I first joined the Southern Christian Leadership Conference to love and admiration for them. Friends have always said, when I would tell them about some of my experiences, "John, you need to put this in a book!" For years I considered doing just that. Finally, when I realized that my experiences were now part of our American history, I felt that it was time to tell my story to a wider audience. I fear that many young people today give little thought to what the young people of the Sixties were doing to make their lives what they are today. I was eighteen when I joined the Civil Rights Movement, and I led even younger people than I into situations where they could be beaten and arrested, or even killed–just so that the young people of today could live in a world that did not treat them differently because of the color of their skin. It's time that these young people today heard some of these stories.

I've been asked why I stepped forward at such a young age, gave up my job and the school program I was in, left my home for the first time in my life, and went on such a dangerous journey. As far back as I can remember, I've always had a passion and caring for people. I respected and honored older people, whether they were my parents, my grandparents, or people I didn't even know. I stood up for the underdog, always putting myself between the child in the playground being bullied and those doing the bullying. I jumped into situations with my heart as well as my head. When I was young, I was always fighting, whether protecting others or protecting myself. The lack of respect shown to my grandmother and mother angered me. It angered me to see people being violated, with their dignity, their spirit, and their humanity taken away.

Growing up in a segregated society, I witnessed the difference between whites and blacks. I saw the difference in schools. The white school looked newer and seemed to be better equipped. Every time I rode by the white school on the segregated bus, that difference bothered me. Little seeds were germinating within my soul as I became aware of all the things that were not right–the things that stripped so many of us of our dignity and needed to be changed. I swore to myself as I got older that I would do something about these conditions, these circumstances.

In the mid-1950's, I became conscious of the Montgomery Bus Boycott taking place less than fifty miles away. I heard about Martin Luther King, Ralph David Abernathy, and Rosa Parks, a woman who grew up about twenty miles from my hometown. Watching the people of Montgomery made me want to do something, and I wished that I was there. I would have been walking the streets at the age of nine if I had been in Montgomery. By the time I got to high school most of the young people I knew were more concerned about today–about dancing, having a good time, and maybe what job they could get. I was thinking about tomorrow. What would tomorrow look like? What would the world be like? And what would my life be like?

So when the opportunity came to fight for freedom, I didn't hesitate. I jumped at the chance. When SCLC sent workers to my hometown to register black people to vote, I realized that with an organization behind me, I could do much more to change lives than if I acted alone. I did not give much thought to my future, because it was not about me–it was about others. It was not about "what I would give up." It was about helping others. It was about my grandmother and my mother. It was about the stranger. It was about a generation that had not yet been born that I needed to fight for. It was about respect. It was about dignity. It was about hope.

Another reason for joining the Movement and jumping into it with my whole heart was that I felt it was a calling, a calling from God. I had gone to church all of my life and had heard about the work of God. Now I felt God calling me to join Him. Calling me to join hands with Him and do His work. To offer hope and dignity to folks. To do His work here and now. Not only would I be a disciple of Martin Luther King, but I would be a disciple for God. Fighting for His children.

I was young back in the 1960s. In 2012, I am old. But I still like and appreciate a good fight. When I look at the Occupy movement, I think it is a good fight–they are standing up today as we did back in the 60s. They are raising the question of poverty and wealth and how that wealth should be distributed, as we did. Shouldn't we all benefit from the wealth in this country that now benefits only a few? I hope this movement will continue to grow. If it does, everyone will benefit. And if this old warrior can give them a hand, I surely will.

I will be forever grateful to Martin Luther King, Jr. for inviting me to join him and his organization, the Southern Christian Leadership Conference. *The Fight for Freedom* describes my experiences during almost seven years with SCLC. I was honored every time I was deployed to a new battlefield in the fight for freedom. I was honored to serve with all of the other freedom fighters–not only my colleagues in SCLC, but also those working with SNCC, CORE and NAACP, as well as those grass-roots leaders across the country that I had the pleasure of working with.

Even though times are not as turbulent today as they were in the 60s, sometimes we have to make sacrifices and suffer if we are to have justice and freedom, as the Occupy movement reminds us. We cannot be silent and sit on the sidelines. I hope this book does something to remind us that sometimes we have to lift our voices and stand up and fight in order that justice and freedom can be a reality for all.

Life on a Plantation

My story has to begin with my maternal grandmother, Susie Ginyard, the strong, loving, dominant figure in my life while growing up. Susie was born in 1894 in Bullock County, Alabama. A single mother, at the age of thirty she moved to Pike County with her children, hoping for a better life in the farm country outside the city of Troy, where cotton, peanuts, and sugar cane were grown in the rich red clay. Troy was the county seat of Pike County, located in the southeastern section of the state and named after Gen. Zebulon Pike of New Jersey, a soldier in the War of 1812, an explorer who discovered Pike's Peak in Colorado, and to the best of my knowledge, a man who never set foot in Alabama.

Susie soon found work on the plantation of Walter Curtis. She and her young children lived on the Curtis plantation in a house that was a little bigger and little nicer than most of the houses occupied by black families in that area. The house was on a quiet, unnamed country road with no neighbors in sight. The closest black family lived a couple miles away. The house sat back a little from the road, surrounded by fields. Next to the red dirt driveway stood a large oak tree with hanging moss. Several large pecan trees towered beside the house. The house had five rooms–a living room, a kitchen, and three bedrooms. The large living room had a fireplace which heated the front part of the house. A wood stove in the kitchen also provided heat and was where food was cooked. Behind the house were an outhouse and a chicken coop.

The mother of seven children, Susie was the matriarch of the Ginyard family. She was like a hen with young chicks. She protected and guided her flock, which in time included grandchildren. Of middle height and slightly overweight, she was dearly loved by her family. In spite of her difficult life, she was easy-going and joyful. She was the heart and soul of the growing family. Her strength came through her faith. She was a strong believer in God and the power of God. She often said, "God can make a way out of no way."

Susie was a faithful church-goer. Almost nothing would stop her from going to church. She went to church on Sundays and then would often return later that night. I remember many summer nights when revival meetings were held during the week that I would have to accompany her on the two or three mile walk to church. We would talk on the way and she would tell me stories. Often under the darkness of night, we would take a shortcut to church through the pastures, laughing and telling each other, "Watch your step!" One night during a revival meeting, I had fallen asleep while the guest pastor was preaching. I was awakened just in time to hear the preacher ask me whether I believed in God. What was a thirteen year old boy to say in front of his faithful grandmother, but "Yes, I believe." Before I knew it, I was a member of her church.

Life was not easy for my grandmother, and she struggled to raise her seven children on her own. She gave most of her children Biblical names. The oldest was Moses (known as Lee), then Aaron (Buck), Esther (Sister), my mother Mattie (Honey), James (Jabbo), Elijah (E.L.), and the youngest, Nora Pearl (Pearl). Susie worked in the fields with her children for years until she was physically unable to do it any longer, and then she began to do domestic work for the Curtis family.

Most of her seven children worked on the Curtis plantation for a good part of their lives, although a couple of them were able to escape the hardship of field work at an early age. Uncle Lee was able to get away by going into the service and settling in Florida instead of returning to Troy. The two youngest, Pearl and E.L., felt that there had to be something better than living the rest of their lives on the five dollars a day they would get working in the fields or doing domestic work. My grandmother saw the truth of what they were saying, and when Pearl reached eighteen years of age, she let her move to Florida to live with Lee. She persuaded E.L. to stay, however, to help support the family. While in Florida, Pearl met her future husband Mitch, a career military man. After they were married, she had the opportunity to see more of the world, living in the different places where he was stationed, including Germany for awhile.

I was the third of Susie Ginyard's many grandchildren. I was born in the hospital in Troy on November 2, 1946, the oldest child of my parents, Henry and Mattie Lue Reynolds. I almost did not make it into the world. My mother had difficulty delivering me, and I had to be pulled from her womb with forceps and suffered deep dents on each side of my head. My difficult birth foreshadowed the difficulties to come in my life.

Life for my parents meant working hard on the plantation, and early on it seemed as if that would be my future as well. My mother, a tiny woman just over four feet tall, worked in the fields on the Curtis plantation, as did my father, who at first was a day laborer but later became a sharecropper. He began sharecropping because he thought he would be able to make more money to provide for his family. Men earned five to seven dollars a day as day laborers. Women made even less, usually no more than four dollars a day. Children only made around two dollars a day.

My father borrowed money from Mr. Curtis to lease land on the Curtis plantation, and he began to work for himself. However, it was not really for "himself" because he was not in control of selling the cotton he raised. Mr. Curtis would pick up the cotton that my father had harvested and bring it to the cotton gin where it was sold. My father never knew how much the cotton truly earned because Mr. Curtis kept the books. He was dependent on Mr. Curtis to be fair and honest with him. But no matter how hard he worked, my father was always in debt at the end of the year. The expense side of the ledger, which included the repayment of the loan from Mr. Curtis, was always greater than the revenue. It was a vicious cycle. My father did this for two or three years until he realized that he would never make it on this or any other plantation. He finally got the courage to say that he wasn't going to do it anymore, and he left the plantation.

And it did take courage for a man to leave the plantation, because few other options were available. Jobs for black men in a segregated society were extremely limited. Troy had no major industry, so most blacks labored in the fields, picking cotton and chopping peanuts. Eventually, however, my father found work as a laborer in the construction field, and he and my mother moved into a small house in the city of Troy. We lived there for two or three years, but unfortunately, when I was about seven years old, my parents separated and I moved with my mother and two younger sisters, Mattie Jean and Susie, to my grandmother's home on the Curtis plantation.

My grandmother still had three of her children living with her: Jabbo, E.L., and Pearl, who had not yet left. When eight people live in one house, it means that you have to share rooms, or even share beds. I slept in a room off the kitchen with my Uncle E.L. Pearl slept in the room with my grandmother until she left for Florida, and then my youngest sister Susie moved in with Grandma. My mother and my sister Matt slept in the living room. Jabbo had the third bedroom.

I had a number of chores around the house. Early in the morning, I collected wood for both the kitchen stove and the fireplace, and then I started a fire in the fireplace. When my mother or grandmother washed clothes, they did this in the yard in a large metal pot with legs. I would collect coals from the fireplace, carry them out to the yard in a metal container, and place them under the pot with some wood to start a fire. The fire would heat the water in the pot to boiling and then the clothes would be put in the boiling water. One day, while carrying the hot coals, a coal fell in my shoe and I was unable to get the shoe off to remove it. I wound up with a severe burn on my right foot which to this day still bears the scar. For months while it healed, my sisters would tease me. They made up a song, "Here comes John with his rotten foot" which they would sing as I cried.

On the plantation it was expected that the parents, the children, and even the grandchildren would work in the field. That was true whether you were a boy or a girl, but boys were definitely expected to work. We were viewed as labor tools, not much else, and that's the way we were treated. My mother put me into the fields to work at the age of nine. I chopped peanuts from late spring to summer. In late summer to early fall, I picked cotton. As I picked the cotton, I would put it into a large bag. Because we got paid by the pound, it was important to stuff as much cotton as possible into each bag. Even as a nine-year old boy, I would be dragging a bag stuffed with forty to fifty pounds of cotton behind me. After the cotton crop was picked, then it was time to cut sugar cane. I used a machete to cut the cane.

I missed a lot of school because of having to work in the fields. I would go and register for school on the first day, but it might be months before

I was able to return to the classroom. Both my two sisters and I worked in the fields, but the burden was lighter on them. They were able to go to school sooner and more often than I could. But it was important for my family that I work, and I realized this. I respected my mother for working so hard to provide for us, and I did my best not to add to her problems.

Often I could hear my mother or grandmother in bed crying because there was not enough food to feed all of us. But then, somehow Uncle Buck would know that we needed help and would walk the three or four miles from his house to ours to bring us food. My grandmother knew that once again, "God had made a way out of no way." I will always be thankful to Uncle Buck for all he did for our family. Even though he and his wife had many children of their own, he always made sure that we did not go without. He continued doing this even after my grandmother died, and Jabbo, E.L., and Pearl had left. My mother, my sisters, and I remained in the little house in the country by ourselves, but we always felt secure knowing that Uncle Buck would be there if we needed him.

Even today, I have powerful images of that period. Black people were exploited and were considered little more than commodities. We worked from sun up to sundown, and if we were lucky, we had an hour off for lunch. We tilled in the hot sun and struggled to get the work done when the weather was cold. I remember once being dragged behind a pickup truck. Mr. Curtis had come to the field to drive us home for lunch. He would pick us up an hour later and bring us back to the field. That day he was in a hurry and figured the sooner he got us home, the sooner we would be back at work. I was just about to get into the back of the truck when he took off without checking to see if we were all on. I held on to the rear bumper and although I tried to pull myself into the back of the truck, I couldn't. As I was being dragged through the red dirt in the field, my mother and Uncle E.L. beat on the top of the cab, trying to get Mr. Curtis to stop. Finally I had to let go. I was more angry than afraid. I realized in that moment that Mr. Curtis didn't really care about us, and I determined then that this life would not be my future. The incident reinforced the anger and humiliation that I felt for what my grandmother had to endure.

One of the domestic jobs that my grandmother performed for the Curtis family was to wash their clothes. Usually, this was done in their yard in the same way that she washed our clothes at home. A large pot was set over a fire and the clothes were heated to a boil. After that they were transferred to a wash tub filled with cold water. My grandmother would then hand wash the clothes in the cold water. Usually during the winter it was in the mid-thirties, but sometimes early in January the temperature would be at or below freezing and the cold water would form icicles. As a child, I often watched my grandmother while she washed the Curtis' clothes, and one day as her hands came up out of the cold water, I saw icicles forming on her fingers. That was my impression as an eight or nine-year-old child, although I'm aware that some might ask, "How is that possible?" But that was what I remember seeing, and that image remains with me even today. I loved my grandmother and felt she deserved more consideration and compassion from her employers.

These two incidents made me angry, and I wished that somehow we could get out of this hell that we found ourselves in. I knew that I was not the kind of person to smile and be agreeable when unpleasant things were done to me. Unfortunately, many black men, including my father, had to do that in order to survive. But even at that age, I had a temper and reached a boiling point very quickly. At school, my nickname was "Big Crook" because of my temper, and I was often in fights. I knew I would be in danger as I grew older because sooner or later I would react unwisely to a white man who was disrespecting me.

I saw how Mr. Curtis treated my Uncle Buck. Buck was a strong man with a large family, and Mr. Curtis exploited him. Mr. Curtis knew that he would work hard to provide for his family, so he gave him tasks that normally would take the strength of two or three men. Mr. Curtis expected all of my uncle's children to follow him into the fields. He would talk to Uncle Buck about my paternal grandfather, Richmond Reynolds, whom I never knew and had never laid eyes on. My grandfather had a reputation as a ladies' man and according to local legend had ten wives—at the same time! My father's mother, Mandy Hicks, was one of those wives. Mr. Curtis used this story of my grandfather in an attempt to create more laborers. He wanted my uncle to produce more children so that he could have more hands in the field.

Mr. Curtis had three children. Like my mother, he had a son and two daughters. His son, Wayne, and I shared the same birth date, although Wayne was a year older. Since they were our closest neighbors, with the little leisure time that I had, I would often play with Wayne, and occasionally with the girls. But one day, my mother came home and told me that I could no longer go to the Curtis' home and play with the children. I asked why, but she just said, "You can't anymore." I kept pushing for a clearer answer, but for whatever reason she was unable or unwilling to explain. As I grew older, I realized that the answer was that I had reached the age when it was no longer acceptable in the segregated South for a black boy to associate with white children, especially females. I did stay in contact with Wayne over the years. Occasionally when I returned home for a visit, I would stop by his office at Troy State University, where he was a professor.

Because Troy and Pike County were segregated, my sisters and I went to a separate school from the white children in the community. I rode the bus to school with the younger brothers of John Lewis, who was already involved in the Civil Rights Movement and who later became a U. S. Congressman. Not only were John and I from the same town, but we were almost "family." My cousin James Crawley was married to one of John's sisters, and they had several children together before divorcing. I'm not sure that John ever realized the connection since James and I have different last names.

Our school was clearly inferior to the white school that we passed every day in terms of its structure, equipment, and teachers. At the beginning of my junior year in high school, I decided to transfer to the city school in Troy. I felt that the city school for blacks was better academically than the one I had been attending. The city teachers stressed the importance of education, and they motivated and encouraged students to strive for a better life. They were able to do this because they were not intimidated, as were the teachers in rural areas. Many of the rural teachers lived on farms owned by whites in areas where there was Klan activity. Even those who owned their own homes were vulnerable to the threat posed by the Klan outside of the city.

My father stayed in the city of Troy after the divorce. I usually saw him on weekends when I came to Troy to visit him and pick up groceries for my mother. Occasionally, he came out to the country and brought food for us. I looked a lot like my father, except that he was taller and stronger. I looked up to him and valued his guidance and influence. His continued presence in my life was important to me. Unfortunately, at this stage of his life my father did not see the importance of education. He had very little education himself and had gone only as far as the third grade. He had

moved from the plantation and had gotten into the construction trade. To
him, what was important was work and making a living. If I wanted to
get an education, it would be up to me to do it. Although I had begun to
dream of going to college, this was truly a pipe dream.

In transferring schools, I had to use my father's address, which was
within the city limits. Although I usually spent one night a week with
my father or with my Aunt Sister, the reality was that I mostly lived with
my mother about six or seven miles outside the city. Initially, I walked to
school, but fortunately, a young white man who lived a few miles away
would pick me up when he saw me on the road. He worked as a salesman
at one of the car dealers in Troy and was on his way to work a little before
7:00 a.m. each morning. After he had picked me up a couple times on his
way into the city, he offered to stop at my house and pick me up. When I
left for the Civil Rights Movement, I lost touch with him and don't know
if he stayed in the area or not. I feel badly about that, because what he did
for me was very unusual at the time. White people usually would not pick
up black people walking on the road since it was not socially acceptable
for white people to ride with blacks in a non-work related situation. I
don't know if he received any hostility from other whites about this, but
he continued giving me a ride until I finished high school. This was one of
those times that God was making "a way for me out of no way."

In those days Troy was totally segregated. One of the few white-owned
businesses that blacks could enter was the grocery store. They were not
allowed in restaurants or in most department stores. Even at the movies,
whites sat downstairs, and blacks had to sit in the balcony. Since we worked
all week and went to church on Sunday, Saturday was the only day of the
week that we could go into town shopping and have some fun. We went
to Love Street, a section of downtown where most of the little cafes and
restaurants were owned or operated by blacks. Blacks from all over the
county would go to Love Street to have a beer and dance.

Every Saturday I would walk the six or seven miles to town to visit my
father, but also to go to Love Street. Love Street is where boys would meet
girls and just have a good time. Of course, it was also a place where fights
would break out after people had had a little too much to drink. You had
to keep your wits about you and be aware of what was happening around
you. In those early days I used to love to dance. I would go to a café and
would dance to the music of artists like James Brown and Ike and Tina

Turner. People would often give me money when I danced. They would lay quarters and dollar bills on a table. Since I had very little money, anything extra that I could earn was a blessing. Dancing was a release for me. I could be authentic in those moments. As long as it was fast or up-tempo music, I would dance until I was exhausted.

Near this section of town were some of the grocery stores and other stores frequented by blacks since they could purchase on credit. On many Saturday evenings, my mother and I would begin our long walk back home carrying the few groceries that she could afford to purchase. Most of the time someone would see us and give us a ride, not always all the way home but at least part of the way. For rural blacks, these few hours were their only escape from the labor that they had endured all week. Love Street was a place where they could let down. It was a time that they could share with friends and family. It was a time to relax.

My grandmother and my parents, who worked so hard and were often tired, couldn't stop just anywhere to have a decent meal or even quench their thirst. There was a really good BBQ restaurant in Troy, but black folks couldn't go into the restaurant, although they could go to a window in the back and try to get an order. But in most instances, they just got the bones, either because that is all they would sell to blacks or because the bones were all that blacks could afford. Many nights I would hear my grandmother and my mother talking about how good the meat was that was left on the bones. And as I lay there, listening to them, it made me angry that they couldn't go in, sit down, and enjoy themselves. I made a vow that someday I would eat at this restaurant. So whenever I came home while I was in the Civil Rights Movement, I made it a point to go to this restaurant on behalf of my grandmother. She died before the Civil Rights Act was passed, so she was unable to ever set foot inside the restaurant.

My grandmother went to Florida in 1961 to visit Uncle Lee. Normally she did not travel and she had never visited her children in Florida before that trip. I often wondered whether she knew that she was ill, because two days after she arrived in Florida, she had a major stroke and never made it back home.

Pike County was a difficult place for blacks to live during those years. In addition to the lack of jobs, there was also the constant fear that blacks faced. When I was downtown walking on the sidewalk, if I met a white woman coming towards me from the opposite direction, I would have to cross the street in order not to catch her eye. This was true for most black men, and it was especially true for men my father's age. For my father, the fear was real. The possibility of being tossed in jail or beaten was an everyday reality for him. Although it was not as dangerous as living in Lowndes County, Troy was still not an easy place to live. Not an easy place to grow up. Not an easy place to have dreams and hopes for the future. We couldn't even go to the library and escape to another world. We were just shackled to this dark world that we had come to know.

It was this life in Troy, Alabama, that made me angry, that made my blood boil. This was taking place during the Cold War when Russia was the enemy, and yet I knew that a white person from Russia would have more rights in Troy than I did. I knew that something had to be done. Someone had to stand up. Someone had to fight for the rights and the dignity of black people in my hometown. Someone had to shine a light into this darkened world. And I asked myself, *Why not me?*

Change Comes to My Hometown

I woke up on a bright summer day in early June. I remember that it was early June because it was a few days after my father's birthday, June 1. There was hardly a cloud in the sky that summer morning, and it was still, not even a breeze moved the air. The rhythm of Troy seemed the same as always. I had no premonition of what was in store for me that day.

My life was looking up. I had escaped the hardship of the plantation, having gotten a job a few weeks before as a custodian at Troy State College, and I was staying in town with my father and his wife Patsy most of the time. With my father's help, I had just bought my first car, a black and yellow 1956 Chevy BelAir, from the salesman who had given me a ride to school from my home in the country for a couple of years. I was also attending a summer program in Troy sponsored by Tuskegee Institute for young people considering college. Mrs. Harrison, my favorite high school teacher, had encouraged me to register for the program. Since the classes took place on weekday mornings and wouldn't interfere with my afternoon job at Troy State, I decided to attend.

After class that day in June, I got behind the wheel of my '56 Chevy and started back to my father's house, intending to have lunch, change my clothes, and go to work later in the afternoon. I turned onto Washington Street and started up the hill, not thinking of anything in particular, just looking around, feeling relaxed and enjoying the day. As I neared the peak of the hill, I noticed two people standing in a yard talking. I slowed down because it struck me that something was unusual about the two people, a young white man and an elderly black woman. I realized as I drew closer that what was different was the young man's body language. The way that he was talking to the woman showed a profound respect that was not typical of the way whites usually talked to black people.

I don't know why, but I pulled over to the curb, stopped the car, and just sat there for several minutes until they finished their conversation. As he said goodbye to the woman and headed towards the next house, I opened the door and got out of the car. I called out to him, "Can I speak to you for a moment? Can I ask you a question?" The question hadn't been on my mind as I sat there in the car, but for some reason, there it was on the tip of my tongue. I asked, "Are you some kind of civil rights worker?" This was a huge gamble for me, because if I had misread the situation, I could have put my life in danger just by asking the question. I had no reason to think that he might be a civil rights worker other than the respect that he was showing this woman. Fortunately for me, he responded by saying "Yes, I am" and introduced himself as Daniel Thompson from Cleveland. I asked if he was the only civil rights worker in town. He said that he was not and asked if I would like to meet the leader of the project and learn more about what they were trying to do in Troy. I said, "Yes."

So instead of going to the house next door as he had planned, Danny climbed into the passenger seat of my car and we headed a short distance away to another section of town. On the way, he explained that the Southern Christian Leadership Conference had instituted a summer program called SCOPE–the Summer Community Organization and Political Education project–throughout the South. Legislation for the Voter Registration Act had been introduced, and civil rights organizations were hopeful that it might pass. Six volunteers had quietly come to Pike County and the city of Troy in response to the call put out by SCLC. I had not heard even a rumor of their presence in town and was very curious to hear more about their plans.

The group had set up an office in a building next to the home of Mrs. Johnnie Mae Warren, the matriarch of a middle-class black family. The Warrens had a small in-law apartment in the corner of their yard, and they had offered this building to the SCLC group. The office was in the front of the building, and there were bedrooms off to the side. While the workers were in Troy, this building became known as the "freedom house." Danny took me into the office and introduced me to Leon Gutherz, a white history teacher from New Rochelle, New York, who was serving as the director of the project. We talked for a few minutes about their plans for the voter registration campaign, and he explained that when I met Danny, he had been canvassing the black neighborhoods.

After we had talked for awhile, Leon said that they could use my help if I was willing to volunteer. They were particularly in need of people who had cars, but they also needed help with other things, such as canvassing. I was thrilled at the opportunity to do something, because I felt that changes were badly needed in Troy. I agreed to do whatever I could, but I had to figure out when I could manage it. Although I was free in the evenings, I wasn't sure how much time I would have during the day between my summer studies and work.

After my conversation with Leon, I walked back towards my car. As I drove along, I thought about what he had said and wondered if change was about to come to Troy. Was change about to come in my life? Would I be the same as I was before I met Danny? As all of these thoughts ran through my head, I suddenly realized that I hadn't been driving the car that day. God had directed my route onto Washington Street and up the hill just in time to see the young white man and the elderly black woman deep in conversation.

I had acted on my own the year before. I had been working in a pool hall in town, racking pool balls and shining shoes. One day in the pool hall, listening to the radio, I heard on the news that the Civil Rights Act had just passed in Congress. At noon, as I sat there trying to decide what I would do for lunch, it hit me. Why walk all the way to Love Street when there was a lunch counter in the drug store only two doors down from the pool hall, and I now had a legal right to eat there. I got up and walked over to the drug store.

As I walked in and sat down on one of the stools at the counter, everyone was stunned by my action. I heard a couple of the women seated further down the counter gasp. The waitress asked me, "What are you doing, boy?" I responded, "I am here to have lunch." She got the owner and they asked me again what I was doing. I said, "I want to be served." The owner turned to his regular customers and announced that he was closing the store. As the lights were turned off, I sat there in the dark for a few minutes, watching everyone leave the store. Since it was clear that they wouldn't serve me, I left and moved on to another drug store. Once again, I requested to be served. This time they weren't sure how to respond. Should they serve me? If so, should they serve me on plates and with silverware as they served their white customers? They finally decided to serve my hamburger and fries on a paper plate, shoving the food towards me on the counter.

The flame had been burning within me for some time. Ten years earlier, as an eight-year old, I had heard on the radio the voices of Martin Luther King, Jr. and Ralph David Abernathy, the leaders of the Montgomery Bus Boycott, which took place only fifty miles from Troy. I thought that they were the most courageous people I had ever heard of. Now, in the summer of 1965 at the age of eighteen, I was ready. I was ready to follow in their giant footsteps. I didn't know what lay ahead. I just knew that I needed to do something.

So I told Leon that I would do whatever I could to help them out. This was an opportunity to really accomplish something to make life better for the people of Pike County. Rather than being a lone soldier in this fight, sitting at a lunch counter on my own, I would be part of a larger group with a strategy. I could learn from them how to organize and motivate people for a longer and more difficult fight. This was an opportunity to bring about change–change in the lives of people and change in the community.

The deputy project director was Frechettia Ford, a nurse from Robbins, Illinois, who served as the administrator for the project. She was a light-skinned black woman, very smart and very capable, whom I admired because of the strength of her beliefs and convictions. I sometimes helped Frechettia in the office, printing the handbills used in the canvassing, since she needed someone with muscles to work the mimeograph machine. I soon got to know the other volunteers working on the voter registration campaign in Troy. Norma Danels and Ned Moore were from Los Angeles, and later Elizabeth Shamburger, a white teenager from Alabama, joined the group.

As I began to work with Leon and the others, going to churches and canvassing neighborhoods, reaching out to people in the hope of getting them to stand up for themselves, I realized that I, too, needed to make some decisions. I had to determine what kind of sacrifices I was willing to make. I had to decide whether to continue to participate in the Tuskegee summer program and evaluate how important that program might be for my future. I also had to decide whether I was willing to give up my job as a janitor at Troy State College to spend more time on the project. Since I had escaped the hardship of the plantation and had gotten this job, my future had been looking better. Did I want to give all this up? This was a big decision for an eighteen-year old, and I wrestled with it for some time.

But as I continued to work with the group, I realized that I needed to commit myself. I needed to commit myself to this fight. The first sacrifice I made was to give up the Tuskegee program. As we began to organize and I became more involved, I came to the realization that I had something to offer and should take advantage of this opportunity. So fairly soon I made the decision that I would give my all to the project. I would give up my job and my opportunity for an education if it would help make a difference in the lives of people.

For me, an eighteen-year old who wasn't planning to leave Troy and migrate to the North, to make a decision to sacrifice everything for a cause was unusual, both in my community and in most communities in Alabama. I felt a responsibility to the members of my extended family who were suffering indignities and humiliation. But I also felt a responsibility to the black people of Pike County. People had come into the county to help black people stand up for themselves. Even though I was young, I felt an obligation to stand up and work with the volunteers who had come to assist us. Making a small sacrifice was worth the cost for the larger good. If we were successful and black people were registered to vote, change would come and life would be better for all of us.

Most blacks in the segregated society of Troy and Pike County were fearful. Black people had to walk a narrow line and be very careful to stay "in their place." Blacks in rural areas who lived on land owned by whites were especially vulnerable since they were beholden to the land owners. The few that were able to own land and their own homes were still vulnerable. Blacks who had moved away from the farms and gotten other jobs also had to walk this narrow line. All blacks were susceptible to the whims of the white power structure, and they were careful not to act in any way that would upset the whites in the community. They were afraid to do anything that might endanger what little they had.

Although 11,000 black people in Pike County were eligible to vote, fewer than 500 were actually registered. A voter registration day was held on the last Monday of every other month at the county courthouse in

Troy. Once or twice a year a special voter registration might be held with registration taking place three or four days in a row. Some of the reasons for the low black registration, besides their fear of going to register, were the literacy tests, which were not easy to pass, and the poll tax, which also discouraged them. We had to work with these major hurdles as we went forward with voter registration in the summer of '65.

One of the most important things that the group needed to do was to reach out to the black community and make them aware that volunteers had come to Pike County to help them register to vote. We had to let them know that someone was there to support them in this effort. With that in mind, one of our early tasks was to go out and canvass different neighborhoods all over the county, which is what Danny Thompson was doing the day I met him. He was talking to people in the black community and identifying who was registered and who was not, so that we would have a better sense of where we needed to focus our effort. We knew that there was no single area we could ignore and that it would have to be a county-wide effort, so we also set up an office in Brundidge, Alabama, the second largest city in Pike County.

We wanted to reach as many people as we could in order to register the largest possible number of people in the county. We needed to educate people about their rights to register to vote and to inform them when registration days would be held. Most blacks did not know that registration took place the last Monday of every other month. One of our objectives was to change this pattern and pressure the county to increase the number of days that voter registration took place.

The best way to reach out to the community was through mass meetings. But in order to have mass meetings, we needed facilities large enough to hold a good sized group of people. We obviously could not use the public schools. A possible option was the two or three black-owned funeral homes. However, churches were the most logical choice, because they were the predominant institutions that blacks owned and controlled. But our early attempts to find churches willing to allow us to hold mass meetings were met with resistance. Even so, the staff would divide up on Sunday mornings and visit different churches. We introduced ourselves to the congregation so that they would know who we were and hopefully we would have an opportunity to say a few words. If we were lucky, we might get a meeting with the pastor or the deacons so that we could make a request to use their church for a meeting.

On the first Sunday after the volunteers arrived in Troy, Leon, Norma, and Frechettia attended service at St. Paul's AME Church, and Ned and Danny attended service at the First Baptist Church. At the AME church, Leon and Frechettia were able to speak to the congregation about their reason for being in Troy. Afterwards, they mingled with the congregation and were able to identify a few people who might be helpful to our efforts, one of whom was the only black contractor in town.

The City of Troy had hired two black policemen just a month before the staff volunteers arrived in town. These officers had limited authority and power and could only work within the black community. They could not stop or question whites, particularly white women. The power structure in Troy used these officers to intimidate those blacks who were assisting in the voter registration efforts. The officers went to the home of Mr. Baker, where Norma Danels was staying. They told him that there had been a bomb threat to First Baptist Church, where he served as a deacon, and warned him that if he did not get Norma out of his home, he would lose his job. They also went to see him at work and told him again that he would be fired unless he got the volunteer out of his home.

This kind of intimidation became fairly common as the project went on. However, because of the threats, Norma decided to return home to Los Angeles. She did not want to be responsible for someone getting hurt or killed because of her presence, and she could not handle the pressure of that responsibility. I don't think that Norma had really understood what Alabama was like before she signed up for the SCOPE project. She didn't realize how difficult it would be for her and the kind of reactions she would get from the white community. I was sad to see her go, but we all felt that it might be best for her and the project if she left Troy, because the pressure was not going to lessen and the possibility was that it might increase.

Norma's situation was somewhat different from that of Elizabeth Shamburger, the young white girl from Alabama, who had come to Pike County after initially working in another county. Reverend Daniel Harrell, the area supervisor for SCLC, had reassigned Elizabeth to Pike County since it was considered safer than many other counties in Alabama. Even so, he wanted her to keep a low profile. He did not want the authorities to know that she was from Alabama, so he assigned her to the smaller city of Brundidge. In Troy she would have been under more scrutiny by the police department or the sheriff's office, which would have made it more likely they might discover that she was from Alabama. This would have put her in serious jeopardy. In some ways Elizabeth was more vulnerable than any of us, because if it was discovered that she was from Alabama, she would have been looked upon as a traitor to the white race. She clearly would have been a target for the Ku Klux Klan.

Even though I was concerned about my own safety, at the time I didn't think about the danger that Elizabeth was facing. I didn't think about the courage that it must have taken for her to be out there with us, working to make life better for black people. At that point in my life, I had been conditioned not to look a white woman in the face, so it was not easy for me to become friends with Elizabeth even though we were close in age. I regret now that I did not try to bridge the gap and get to know her–to hear her story and learn what gave her the strength to stand up for what she believed was right. Since she was from Alabama, I think she must have understood the cultural divide that kept us from truly getting to know each other, even though we were soldiers together in the fight for freedom. I know that I respected her, and I appreciated her sacrifice and the fact that she was willing to put everything on the line, even her life.

Our group recruited young people in the black neighborhoods to help in our canvassing efforts by handing out flyers. This was important to the overall goal of the project, and the young people were able to canvass a larger area than the adults could in the same amount of time. Also, we thought it was a good idea to get the young people educated about voter registration and involved in what we were doing. Hopefully, they would share the information with their family and friends. Unfortunately, the young people often ran into harassment and intimidation. On a number of occasions, unidentified white men or the two black officers would follow them. Although we were concerned, we were not going to let this intimidate us. As a safety measure, we recruited more young people so they could work in teams and watch out for each other.

In addition to scheduling mass meetings in churches in the city, we wanted to have meetings in the rural areas of Pike County as well. One of the first rural churches that we visited was Beulah Hill Baptist Church in Banks, the closest town to Troy. Reverend Manley, the pastor, had indicated his willingness for us to have a mass meeting at the church, which seated about 125 people. My first arrest in the Civil Rights Movement occurred on the day that Leon, Frechettia, and I went to Beulah Hill Baptist Church to prepare for a mass meeting to be held that evening, July 15, 1965.

Our plan was to go first to Brundidge to meet some people at a church and arrange for mass meetings there. But on the way to Brundidge, I had an accident, skidding through an intersection and knocking down a stop sign. Although no one was injured, my car ended up on an embankment, stuck on the stop sign pole. Some white men in a truck pulled up and asked if we needed help. As is customary in the South, they had guns on the gun rack in the back. Since we were a mixed group, we were cautious and refused their assistance. We were finally able to get a ride from a young black man who took us to Brundidge for our appointment. Leon, Frechettia, and I made a collective decision that we would all go to Brundidge and would not leave anyone behind to stay with the car. Since the accident had taken place on a rural, isolated road with little traffic, we feared if it was discovered that we were civil rights workers, the person left behind could be in danger. Even though I was breaking the law by leaving the scene of an accident, we decided it was worth the risk. Experiences in the past had shown that civil rights workers dare not take the chance of being in vulnerable situations. There certainly had been other incidents throughout the South where civil rights workers had been killed in similar circumstances.

After our appointment, someone drove us back to the scene of the accident, so that we could try to get the car off the embankment. But when we arrived, we saw that the police had arrived as well. After closely questioning us, I was taken to jail and charged with leaving the scene of an accident, and the car was towed back to Troy. After a few hours, I was able to pay the $48 fine and was released. Although I may not have been arrested because of civil disobedience, the arrest had been the result of my civil rights activities. So going to jail for the first time was a privilege and was the initiation for the fifteen or more arrests to come while I was with SCLC. Frechettia and Leon went on to Beulah Hill Baptist Church that evening and had a good turnout for the first of our many mass meetings in Pike County.

We felt that the current schedule of voter registration, one day every other month, was not going to be sufficient to handle the number of people that we anticipated would turn out through our efforts. Leon went to the courthouse to talk to Malcolm Gilchrist, the Chief Registrar, about the possibility of having additional registration days to give more people an opportunity to register to vote. The Chief Registrar was reluctant to add more days for two reasons. An open registration had already been held in Troy just before the arrival of the SCLC staff. Also, he did not agree with Leon that many blacks would turn out.

This attitude was typical of many whites, who believed that they knew what blacks were thinking and how they would act. He assumed they were not interested in registering. But I felt that he was wrong. His assumption may have been true of the older generation, but I did not believe that he knew how younger blacks would respond. He definitely didn't know me and how I felt. He didn't know that I was from Troy and that I was very angry about how we had been mistreated. I knew that if I felt this way, there must be others in Pike County, especially professional blacks, who felt the same way and would come forward and try to register. At our mass meetings we would be stressing the impact that a large black vote could have on their lives. Leon persisted with his demand, saying that it was the Chief Registrar's responsibility to register the people that we delivered. He told him that we would make sure there would be enough people to justify the added days. The Chief Registrar said that he would have to get permission from the State to add more days. Leon told him to do whatever was necessary. We soon got the additional days.

We had several mass meetings to prepare people for the voter registration. We were concerned about the literacy test that people would have to take and wanted to prepare them for it. Reverend Harrell, SCLC's area supervisor, was raised in Alabama and still lived there. He was familiar with the attitude of many blacks, particularly of my father's generation, who felt that they were not bad off, that the white people in Pike County were fairly good to them, and life was not as harsh as in some other places. Rev. Harrell was concerned that they might be somewhat reluctant to register, so he wanted to speak at some of our early mass rallies. He spoke a couple days before the first scheduled registration date. He told them that even if they were not personally being brutalized, they were being held back in many ways. He urged them to register to vote.

On the first registration day, about seventy people showed up. Three registrars were on duty, but throughout the whole day, only forty people were processed. And of that forty people, only nine were able to pass the literacy test. We had set up a process to monitor the registration. We gave people numbers and checked them in by recording their name and address. Once they had gone through the process, they came back and let us know if they had passed the test or not. If they had failed, they told us the reason they had been given for not passing the test. We were able to keep track of how many people were actually processed and how many people were turned away without having an opportunity to go through the process. We combined the number of people who had failed the test and were thereby turned away and the number of people who never got through the process because of the slow pace of the registrars. This would provide important information for us later.

We knew that the registrars were processing as few people as possible so they could say there were not enough people to justify the additional voter registration days. We needed to produce even more people so that the registrars could not possibly handle in one day the number of people that were actually there to register. For a while, we put up with the registrars' slow pace, but soon realized that at this rate we would only be able to register a few hundred people during the entire summer. Hosea Williams, Director of the SCOPE project for all of the southern states, had instructed SCLC staff not to conduct marches unless absolutely necessary. But we finally decided that we had put up with the registrars' stalling tactics long enough, and something more needed to be done.

Leon went to Ben Reeves, the probate judge, to complain about the registrars. Leon told him that we would start marching in the streets or call a boycott if the process failed to improve. Judge Reeves was popular, both in the white community and the black community. He owned one of the few grocery stores downtown where blacks frequently shopped because they were able to buy food on credit. The black community viewed Judge Reeves as being different from most white men in the county power structure. He was reasonable, someone they could talk to if they ran into trouble. He was one of the few white people who would listen and try to help them. Politically Judge Reeves was a moderate. Even the white community who voted him into office knew he was not an extremist. In one of our meetings with him, he commented that keeping the Klan from getting too powerful in Pike County was a priority for him.

Not unlike the black community, the power structure of Troy was fearful. They did not want Troy and Pike County to become another Selma where there had been so much violence and people had been killed. Judge Reeves was concerned about this, and the Sheriff and the Police Chief were as well. Leon used this fear effectively. They were nervous about what Leon might do, especially after Leon, Mrs. Warren, and I led a march of about 300 people on the Courthouse.

Troy, like many southern cities, has a square in its downtown area. In the center of the square is a small park with a bandstand, used for public gatherings and musical events. In the days before malls were built on the outskirts of town, the square served as the hub for people coming to town for business or shopping. There were two department stores, a bank, a drugstore, and several other businesses located on the four streets that formed the square: Three-Notch Street was on the west, Elm Street on the north, South Oak Street on the east, and Church Street on the southern side of the square. The courthouse and jail were on Church Street, a couple blocks from the square.

We wanted to show the power structure that we were serious about the business of registering people and that we could produce more than enough people to keep the registrars extremely busy. We had talked and reasoned with them. Now we needed to put our bodies in the street. We gathered early one morning at St. Paul's Church, a couple miles from the downtown square, for the first of three marches that we would conduct over the summer. After praying at the church, we formed a double line and began to march to the courthouse. We had decided that we would not march in the street and disrupt traffic, but instead would march on the sidewalk. As we got closer to downtown, we turned left and headed towards Elm Street which led us into the square. We marched around the square and then turned right on Church Street and headed towards the courthouse. As we entered Church Street, we moved off the sidewalk and continued our march in the street. We had been silent up to this point, but then we began to sing so that those in the courthouse and those housed in the county jail would know we were coming.

Once we arrived at the courthouse, we formed a single line and entered the main door and headed down the corridor to the room that the Chief Registrar had set up for voter registration. Because of our numbers, only about a third of us were able to get into the building. The remainder stayed in line outside on the street. The Chief Registrar had increased the number of registrars to four. But with all of these people to process, the registrars could see that they were going to have a long day, no matter whether they continued to slow the process down as they had been doing or whether they registered people as quickly as they could.

A mix of people had marched with us that morning. There were people from Troy, from Brundidge, and from some of the smaller towns, such as Banks. There were people from the farms and plantations. Some of the people were educated, and some were illiterate. We had held a number of mass meetings the previous evening in order to prepare people for this day. We organized the line so that the educated people were in front. We felt that they should be able to pass the literacy test, and we would therefore have a good idea early in the day as to how quickly the registrars were processing people. We had demanded that the registrars permit those people unable to read or write to take the test orally, and they had agreed to that. At our mass meeting the night before, we tried to prepare people for the test, and we continued to coach the people in line until they got close to the registrars. The number of people that went through was larger than the previous registration days. But by lunch time, the line was still out the door. At this stage we weren't sure what the success rate would be.

We wanted people who couldn't read and write to be there that day as well, so that we could document how many people were turned away because they couldn't pass the literacy test in spite of taking it orally. Leon had argued with the Chief Registrar and Judge Reeves that the literacy test should be eliminated. Leon told Judge Reeves that he should order the Registrar to discontinue use of the literacy test. We felt that he could take it upon himself to rule against the literacy test as opposed to having it imposed upon them. Leon also threatened to bring in federal registrars so that people who wanted to register could do so. Clearly, we could document how many people were being turned away, and we did in fact contact the Justice Department with the data we had been collecting.

At most of the meetings that Leon had with the county officials, Frechettia or I usually accompanied him. These meetings took place in Judge Reeves' office on the second floor of the courthouse, as opposed to the Chief Registrar's office in a wing on the first floor. If Leon was out of town, then Frechettia and I met with the officials. Since Leon was often invited to other counties to speak and get registration going there, I became a familiar face to the officials in Troy, and they seemed to assume that I was the second in command. On at least one occasion, Judge Reeves called the freedom house and requested a meeting with me to discuss additional days for voter registration. I'm not sure why they thought I was second in command. They may have assumed that because Frechettia was a woman, she couldn't possibly be the second in command, although in fact, she was. Whatever the reason, they assumed that I was the person they should deal with in Leon's absence, and I didn't tell them otherwise. I wanted them to believe that I was an outsider, not just a local teenager. As long as they assumed this, it gave me more credibility in the meetings with them. When I said something, I was taken seriously.

It was at these meetings that I learned the art of negotiating. Leon always sat across the table from Judge Reeves, and I usually sat to Leon's left. I was able to scan the faces of the opposition, and I learned how to read their expressions and get a sense of whether they were being sincere or were playing games with us. This is where I learned about the "other." I learned that you had to listen to the other side and hear what their goals were. This is where I learned that you couldn't let your passion or frustration keep you from seeing and hearing the other side. You had to do this in order to reach an agreement and know if you had a victory or not.

We continued our efforts to bring in as many people as possible to register. One night in the midst of a mass meeting, Leon was explaining to the audience what we were trying to do. But then he paused and said, "I have someone else that you need to hear from, and I want him to speak tonight." When I heard this, I wondered who he was talking about since I knew that no one from out of town had come to speak. Then when he said that this person was someone local who had sacrificed much to help with the voter registration effort, I realized that he was talking about me. Leon and I had never discussed the possibility of my speaking, so I was taken by surprise.

I slowly rose from my seat in the front pew, a little nervous because I had never spoken publicly anywhere before, not even at school. So this was a new experience for me. I stood there for a moment catching my breath, not knowing what I was going to say. But in that moment I knew that God was with me. The words began to flow from my mouth. I knew that it wasn't me, but was God speaking through me. I started off by saying that I knew that I was doing the work of God. I knew that I was walking in the footsteps of Jesus. Jesus had suffered and sacrificed to make life better for people. And that's what I was trying to do in Troy. I said to them, "Do not be afraid. It's time to stand up now. Do not be afraid, for God will take care of you." It was an amazing moment for me.

After that, Leon and I became a team. I was the motivator, and he was the teacher. I began to speak all around the county. Even when Leon went out of town for speaking engagements, I would go with him. Other counties were hearing about Leon and what we were doing in Troy, and so he was being asked to go to other areas in Alabama to speak. Leon would introduce me as "One of your own." In spite of the fact that the black community began to learn that I was a local, the white community still did not realize it.

This assumption that I was one of the outside volunteers was important for me. The local officials did not realize that I was from Troy, probably because they couldn't imagine that anyone from Troy would be bold enough to be as active and outspoken as I was. I used this to my advantage in order to protect my family in the same way that John Lewis had to protect his family. They hadn't connected John with Troy even though he had been beaten severely a few months earlier on Bloody Sunday when Alabama state troopers attacked civil rights marchers on the Edmund Pettus Bridge in Selma. His connection with Troy wasn't known, either in the white community or the black community.

The fact that the power structure did not know who I was gave me leverage after I left town and became a staff member of SCLC. I would use the fact that I was viewed as an outsider to continue to check on activities that were taking place, or not taking place, in Troy. I called Judge Reeves a couple times a month, no matter where I was working in the Movement, just to see what was happening. If progress wasn't being made, I would use the threat that I would come back to town. One of the first issues that I called him about concerned the two black police officers hired by the city. I requested that he meet with the city's police chief and give those officers more authority since it was unfair that they couldn't be full-fledged policemen and enforce the laws on everyone. Years later I visited Judge Reeves in his office and he told me that if they had known that I was from Troy, I would most likely have been killed.

Eventually, my father heard of how much I had gotten involved in the voter registration effort in Troy, and he became upset and fearful. My father had escaped the hardship of the plantation life. He was now living in Troy and owned a home that he had built with a small settlement received from a work-related injury that had resulted in the loss of sight in one eye. He had a good job working as a cement finisher in the construction trade and was making a good income, more money than he had ever had in his life. Life for him was pretty good. But then SCLC had arrived in town and somehow his son had gotten caught up in their activities. Since the white power structure assumed I was an outsider, I felt that no one would connect me to my father, at least that is what I hoped. But as he saw it, my involvement jeopardized everything he had worked for over the last few years. He wanted me to stop what I was doing, but talking to me didn't seem to work. He tried, but couldn't persuade me to stop. His fears grew as I continued to go out, talking to people and bringing them to the courthouse to register to vote.

One night as he questioned me once again about what I was doing, I quietly tried to explain to him that I was trying to make life better for black people. I was fighting for their freedom. Finally, he couldn't take it anymore. Unable to convince me to stop what I was doing, he grabbed a broom and began to beat me with the handle. He beat me with it until it began to splinter into pieces. Then he grabbed the cord from an old broken refrigerator and began beating me with that saying, "You are going to cause me to lose everything. I'm working hard to make a living, but you are just going to ruin everything." I didn't respond as he continued to beat me. I could feel the blood on my back and the welts forming, but I wouldn't challenge him. As he continued to beat me and his shouting got louder, I could hear footsteps coming from the bedroom down the hall. My stepmother, Patsy, ran into the room calling out to my father, "Stop it! Stop it! You're going to kill this boy. You've done enough." I could barely see, but she was pulling his arm. She kept saying to him, "Henry, stop it. Stop it." And finally, the beating ended. She slowly dragged him down the hallway back towards their bedroom. I lay on the floor for a few minutes, crying and in pain–not angry at my father, but sad–sad that he couldn't see that I was trying to make things better for him as well.

As the pain lessened, I began to rise from the floor and slowly got to my knees. After a few more seconds, I pulled myself up and made my way out the door and got into my Chevy. I sat there for a few minutes, trying to decide where to go. I couldn't stay at my father's house any longer. I knew I shouldn't go to my mother's since she would be upset at what had happened. My Aunt Sister lived on the other side of town, and I considered going there. But as I began to drive away, I found myself heading toward the freedom house. As I drove, my father's voice was echoing in my ear, "You're not my son anymore. You're not my son. You have defied me." I heard his words over and over until I reached the freedom house. When Frechettia opened the door, she saw the condition that I was in and asked what had happened, afraid that I had been attacked by a mob. I explained that my father had beaten me. Frechettia, the nurse, took over and she began to tend to my wounds and try to ease the physical pain. Soon, Leon arrived.

As Frechettia continued to work on me, I told Leon about the encounter with my father. I cried when I told him that my father had said I was not his son any more. Then I heard Leon say, "Then I will be your father." I didn't know if I could believe those words, but they were words I needed to hear. I knew the relationship between my father and me was damaged. We were estranged, and I didn't know if the relationship would ever be repaired. Years later I learned from Patsy that my father was so afraid I was going to be killed in the Movement that he took out an insurance policy on my life, so that he would be able to bring my body back home to Troy. His fears were not misplaced, because a number of parents did have to bring their children home from the battlefields of the Movement. I realized then that the beating he gave me was not only because of his fear of losing everything he had worked so hard for, but that he might lose me as well.

Exhausted, I slept the night away, and awoke the next morning knowing what I had to do. I was strengthened in my resolve to give up everything for the fight for freedom. I had now sacrificed my relationship with my father for my commitment to something greater. As Luke 4:18-19 says, "To bring the good news to the poor. To proclaim liberty to the captive. To bring new sight to the blind. And to set the downtrodden free."

We worked at the courthouse during the voter registration all that summer. Since there was no cafeteria there, we usually went to the black section of town for lunch. One day I told Leon and Frechettia about my experience asking to be served at the drug store counters the previous year. So we decided that we would eat at Byrd Drugstore where most of the whites who worked at the courthouse had lunch. We were not welcomed and had difficulty getting served. The owner came over to us and asked us to leave. When we refused, Mr. Byrd said that he would serve his dog before he would serve me. I became angry and said that I intended to be served. I had not yet been trained by SCLC to deal non-violently with these kinds of situations, and I still had trouble keeping my temper under control. Frechettia and another young volunteer calmed me down, and we were eventually served.

Soon we had a major victory. Judge Frank M. Johnson from the Federal Court ruled that the county should stop using the literacy test and poll tax, because it was clear they were using this as a way to discourage black people from registering. Judge Johnson had made significant rulings in Alabama in favor of the Movement. It was Judge Johnson who ruled after Bloody Sunday that Dr. King could march from Selma to Montgomery and ordered protection for the marchers. Once the literacy test was out of the way, we were able to significantly increase our numbers.

At the end of July, I drove Leon and Frechettia to Brundidge for a meeting. Right after we arrived, we received a call from Mr. Gilchrist, wanting Leon to come back to Troy to meet with him, Judge Reeves, and the police chief. They informed Leon that we would have extra days beginning with the next regularly scheduled Monday voter registration, and from then on, we would have extra days each registration week.

Two hundred people were waiting for us to begin registration on August 16, the next registration date. The registrars processed them all. While at the beginning of the summer, we had only seen forty people go through the process, now we saw that number increase to 237 on one day in August and another 260 the next day. In just those two days alone, we registered as many black people as had been registered in Pike County prior to our campaign. This momentum continued for the rest of the project, as we were able to register larger and larger numbers of people.

One person who had come early to register was my stepmother, Patsy Reynolds. Patsy came to support me and told me, "I just want to be here with you." Patsy had disagreed with my father's actions, and this was her way of saying that to me without causing strife between my father and her. She had to make three trips before she successfully registered because the literacy test was still in place the first two times. The third time she walked out of the courthouse with her registration card in her hand and said to me, "Son, I will be back tomorrow with my mother." It would be some years later, however, before my father would register to vote.

My mother came to Troy from the plantation some weeks later to register. People like my mother seldom went to the courthouse unless they were going to court or someone was in jail. But now she was coming to register to vote. I greeted her when she arrived. I don't know what she was feeling at that moment, but I was proud of her. She just gave me a small hug and said, "Boy, how you doin'?" But when she left the courthouse, she had a smile on her face. To see that was worth everything to me. My mother and stepmother represented hundreds and thousands of people who came to the courthouse to register. The people from the plantations and the domestic workers were the most vulnerable, and I was so proud of all those who dared to take a stand. I will never forget all those people who stood so tall that long summer.

Leon began to think about what would happen after the SCLC volunteers were gone, and how progress could continue to be made. He began to plan for an organization that could carry on the work. He wanted to train the group before the project came to a conclusion and the volunteers left Troy. It was decided that the organization should be an integrated group that would work together on issues. Early in August, an organization was formed and officers were elected. The representatives from the black community were Johnnie Mae Warren, Charles Stringer, Brenda Smith, and Charles Terry. The white establishment chose the white representatives. This group was to meet periodically to monitor the progress that was taking place in Troy, in terms of voter registration, education, and employment. The hope was that the organization would continue to work in the community.

As the summer began to wind down, I knew that Leon, Frechettia, Danny, and the others would be leaving. I began to wonder what would happen to me after they left. My father and I were estranged. I had been so committed to what was taking place that summer that I had made the sacrifice of giving up my job and putting off the possibility of going on to school. I had dedicated myself to the Movement that summer, both in body and soul. There was also a sense of sadness that these people that I had come to respect and love would be leaving. Leon felt that I could be a leader in the community if I chose to stay, and he began to contact people at SCLC to see if I could attend SCLC's Citizenship Education School.

I had been fighting for freedom throughout the summer. I knew that I was doing something worthwhile, something greater than me, and I was committed to that fight. I knew that I could not stay in Troy and continue to live the routine life I had been living. It was clear to me that I would have to go somewhere else if I was going to be a soldier in the Movement, for I had been arrested twice by this time, and I knew this was just a prelude to what was to come. I had been beaten by my father's own hand, which prepared me for what I was to face from the hands of the segregationists and police. I knew that this fight was important, and I was willing to make the sacrifice, whatever that might be.

But I knew that joining this fight put my family at risk as well. People, like my mother, who lived and worked on a plantation could be thrown off the land at a moment's notice, losing both their job and their home. This was a common threat that the plantation owners used to "keep blacks in their place." But I was also concerned about the possibility of her being harassed or harmed by the Klan. My mother lived in a rural area with my sisters, about two miles from the closest black family. She was very vulnerable, but I'm not sure she thought about this when she said that she wouldn't stop me from going to SCLC training.

Just before the project was shut down in Troy, I was accepted to the Citizenship Education School at the Penn Center in South Carolina. This would be the first time that I had been away from Troy, and I was nervous about going, even though I would be on my own for only a few weeks. I had grown both personally and educationally through my involvement in the Movement activities that summer. Even though I was shy, I felt that I would be okay and that God would take care of me.

Leon drove me to Selma where I was to catch a bus to the Penn Center. During the drive to Selma, I began to wonder if I would ever again see this man who had become so important to me. We drove along Highway 80 where Viola Liuzzo had been killed. We drove closer and closer to Selma, and then we approached the Edmund Pettus Bridge. This was where Hosea Williams and John Lewis and hundreds of others had been beaten, trampled by horses, and shocked with cattle prods. My nervousness began to rise as I thought of what might lie ahead for me. We drove through the streets of Selma, headed for Brown Chapel where Leon was to drop me off and where I would begin this new journey that would change my life forever. Brown Chapel had been the center of all of the activities in Selma. Seeing it and being there was an honor.

It was finally time for Leon to return to Troy and shut down the freedom house, this place where I had spent so much time, learned so much, and made such good friends. There in front of Brown Chapel, Leon and I hugged and held each other for a long while, and we both began to cry. I stood there on the street in this strange place and watched Leon drive away. And I wondered what was next for me.

A New Life

After Leon dropped me off at Brown Chapel in Selma that morning, I climbed onto one of the two waiting buses and took a seat next to the window. The buses were filling up with people like me who had been chosen to receive the two-week training from SCLC. Finally, the buses rolled away from Brown Chapel and headed for the highway that would lead us to the Penn Center on St. Helena Island, South Carolina, halfway between Charleston and Savannah.

As the bus picked up speed on the highway, I looked out the window thinking about my experiences that summer in Troy, the work that I had done, and what I had lost–my beloved '56 Chevy! Because of what I had been doing, I now had a broken relationship with my father and hadn't seen him in almost two months. As I looked out the window, I could see the image of my father in my reflection. My father and I had always been together, but this time, as I embarked on a new life in the Movement, he wasn't there. But then I thought of Leon and remembered the first time I had seen him, standing in the middle of the Freedom House and I heard again that New York accent of his welcoming me. I began to feel better, knowing how close we had become and what he had come to mean to me. The bus drove for hours down the highway. I wondered what would be next for me, what forks in the road lay ahead and where they might lead. I knew I was about to be trained to teach people to read and write and would learn how to train others to do the same. But beyond that, the future was unknown.

I had no way of knowing that this journey I was embarking upon, with Leon's encouragement, would change my life forever. I had no idea then that I would actually meet the two men whose voices I had first heard on the radio ten years earlier as a young boy. I certainly never imagined that Martin Luther King, Jr. and Ralph David Abernathy–these two men whose courage had so impressed me when they led the Montgomery Bus Boycott in 1955–would become a part of my life. But not only was I about to meet these two men, but for the next seven years I would work for them. The world was literally about to open up for me. This journey that I was beginning would allow me to travel the world, meet a president, and work with celebrities such as Joan Baez and Diana Ross. The dreams, that I hadn't even dared to dream, were about to become a reality. The journey would not be an easy one. It would not be without fear. It would not be without scars. It would mean spending time in jail. But this journey would be the most important journey of my life.

The buses arrived at the Penn Center late that afternoon and pulled up in front of the main building. The Penn Center campus consists of several buildings located on about fifty acres in an area of South Carolina known for its Gullah culture. It is a beautiful campus with massive moss-covered live oak trees. A large hall, classrooms, offices, and a few bedrooms were on the first floor of the main building. Most of the bedrooms, however, were located on the second floor, which is where I would be on this particular occasion. We settled into our rooms and soon began the work at hand, learning the skills we would need to bring back to our communities.

During the training at the Penn Center, I had a surprising and shocking religious experience. As a young boy I had gone to church with my grandmother quite a bit, and some of the older people in the community even felt that I was going to be a preacher some day, although this was not something I had ever considered. But during this experience at the Penn Center, I realized that God was calling me to a new place, calling me to a new service beyond what I had previously considered. In essence, there were two parallel tracks taking place in my life at the same time.

One track was that I wanted to serve the community. I didn't want to go back to being the person I had been before I met Danny Thompson and Leon. In some ways I had been freed. I had found my voice and the courage that I needed. There was a sense of wanting to do more, of not being quiet any longer. I didn't want to be like my father. I knew there must be something more.

The second track was this encounter I had with God. A sort of numbness had come over my body, not paralyzing me, but it was a sensation I had never felt before. Also, there was something like a voice that I heard as this was happening. For a frightening few hours I didn't know what I was experiencing or how to deal with it. I think now that God was talking to me, testing my commitment to the Movement. He was saying, "Are you truly committed to this cause? For if you are, I will always be with you." And God was with me throughout my time in the Movement.

This incident led me to have a conversation with Mrs. Septima Clark, a middle-aged woman from South Carolina who had been very active in Charleston. She had been a teacher for many years in Charleston, but was fired by the Charleston County School Board, in part because of her membership and activity in the NAACP. Mrs. Clark encouraged blacks to go into the teaching profession and was a strong advocate in this effort. When the Charleston School Board fired her, she began to work with those black people on Johns Island, South Carolina, who couldn't read or write. She used a method of teaching people to read and write that she had devised. She was successful in her work on Johns Island and began to be noticed by others outside of South Carolina, including SCLC. Mrs. Clark was brought into SCLC to help run the Citizenship Education Program and to teach others to use her method of teaching on a larger scale throughout the South. Mrs. Clark was a quiet, dignified woman, but also a woman of great power. She was a woman you wanted to spend time with, listen to, and learn from.

I talked to Mrs. Clark over the next few days, not only about the religious encounter that I experienced, but also about my life as a young boy growing up in Troy. I shared with her what I had done during the summer with the SCOPE project. I don't know whether Leon or someone else had forwarded information, but she already had some knowledge of my background and me. Out of these conversations, she saw something in me that she felt could be useful to the Movement and to SCLC, and she talked to Dorothy Cotton, the Director of the Citizenship Education Program, who was also at the Penn Center.

One day near the end of the training program, Mrs. Clark sent someone to my room, asking me to meet with her in the cafeteria. As she and I sat opposite each other at one of the cafeteria tables, she told me that she had made a phone call to Dr. King and recommended to him that I become a member of the SCLC staff. I didn't know what to say. I was overwhelmed and started to cry. No one besides Leon had ever done anything like that for me. I held her hands for several minutes not able to speak. She said that she would bring me back to Atlanta with her so I could meet with Dr. King.

After the program was over, I accompanied Mrs. Clark and Dorothy Cotton to Atlanta in a car loaded with the equipment used for the training sessions. We arrived on a Saturday afternoon and went to the SCLC office on Auburn Avenue and unloaded some of the equipment. They arranged a room for me at the YMCA a couple blocks from the office. I learned later that Dr. King often used the YMCA facilities as a getaway from the stress of running SCLC. Mrs. Clark and Dorothy gave me enough money to get me through the weekend and introduced me to a staff member in the office who lived nearby so that there would be another person I could call upon that weekend.

On Monday I returned to SCLC headquarters. Dr. King was not normally involved in the hiring of staff, but for some reason, Mrs. Clark had called him directly and taken this route of introducing me to SCLC. Usually, Andrew Young and Hosea Williams hired the field staff, and they tended to hire the people they knew or those who were recommended to them by people they knew. Mrs. Clark had a great deal of influence with Dr. King, and she wanted to by-pass the usual procedures to make sure that I became a part of SCLC. She knew that if Dr. King said yes, that was the end of it.

It wasn't until Tuesday afternoon that Dorothy Cotton took me over to Ebenezer Baptist Church, about two blocks from the SCLC office, to meet with Dr. King. We found him in the sanctuary. Dorothy introduced me and gave Dr. King a brief synopsis of my background, where I was from, and the reasons she and Mrs. Clark thought that I would be a good person to work for SCLC, based on what they had seen in me at the Penn Center and the leadership that I had displayed while working on the SCOPE project that summer.

I was extremely nervous and shy, so I don't remember what I said. But I do remember shaking Dr. King's hand and feeling totally in awe that I was actually meeting him. It was a moment that I will never forget, and I knew even then that the moment would be with me forever, no matter what happened. After I had calmed my nerves, I remember that he asked a question of Dorothy and then he asked me if I knew John Lewis. I told him that we had both attended the same school but that I had gone to school with his younger brothers, not him. Then Dr. King asked me two questions. The first was if I believed in, and could accept, the principle of non-violence. I remember saying that I didn't know anything about non-violence, but I was willing to accept it as a tactic. He said that non-violence was important to SCLC and it must also be important to those who worked for SCLC. The other question was whether I was willing to die for what I believed in. Was I willing to die for the Movement? I immediately answered, "Yes."

The latter question was easier for me to answer than the question of non-violence because of the mistreatment of blacks that I had witnessed all of my life. In that moment, I could see my grandmother with frozen hands putting white people's clothes on the line. I understood that it was necessary to sacrifice in order that people might be free, and I was willing to give my life to make that happen. At the end of the conversation, Dr. King told me that if I would read Gandhi and be willing to take some more training, I could join the SCLC field staff. In the meantime, he said I could work around the office, assisting Dorothy with whatever she might need and that he might have some things for me to do as well.

As I left the church, I was thankful that Dr. King had agreed with Mrs. Clark and had hired me. I believe that they both saw my passion and my commitment to the Movement. They knew I was speaking from the heart and had demonstrated over the past few months that I wanted to make a difference. I was relieved to finally have some direction in my life. This was a new beginning, a new life for me. After the encounter with Dr. King, I knew that I was about to help change the South and therefore America. I was officially a part of the staff of the Southern Christian Leadership Conference, one of the most dynamic and powerful organizations of the time. I was about to become a soldier in the fight for freedom and join with other men and women who, like me, were willing to die for what they believed in.

I was about to join Hosea Williams, a true soldier in the fight for freedom who had shed his blood on the Edmund Pettus Bridge in Selma,

Alabama. Hosea had been a soldier in the military as well, having served in World War II in an all-black unit under General George Patton. Hosea had been badly wounded in battle, which earned him a Purple Heart, and he spent a year in a military hospital in Europe. Hosea and Ralph were the two people on the staff who had served in the military.

In some ways I equated SCLC and the military. Those who join the military give up a certain amount of personal freedom, but are willing to sacrifice and to serve. This was also true of those who became staff members of SCLC. We were willing to sacrifice for something larger than ourselves in order to be a part of this movement that was taking place. We had to be willing to give up our jobs and the opportunity to make some money, give up our cars (as I had done), and give up family and friends, at least for a while. When I joined SCLC, I put on a different kind of uniform. I put on a "freedom suit" and I wore it with pride. The freedom suit worn by field staff consisted of jeans, a denim jacket and work boots.

The King/Abernathy Partnership

The day after my interview with Dr. King, I was working downstairs in the building housing the SCLC offices, nervous and excited about being an official SCLC staff member. About mid-morning, as I was coming out of the communication office, suddenly the back door opened and Dr. Abernathy came striding in. I nodded and said, "Good morning," too shy to introduce myself or say anything more. He responded to my greeting and walked into his office across the hall.

My mind flashed back to a time ten years earlier, when I was about nine years old. As a young boy, my family didn't have a television, so we heard the news on the radio. Listening to the radio one day, I heard the voice of a black man, saying "I give this city notice. We are tired, and we're not going to take it anymore." "Wow!" I said, never having heard a black man say such things. I had heard that something was happening in Montgomery, just fifty miles up the road from Troy. The adults in my family were talking about a black woman in Montgomery who had refused to give up her seat on a bus and had been tossed into jail. Even though I was old enough to have felt the pain of racism, I wondered why the police would put the woman in jail. I learned that black people were not riding the buses any longer. Although I didn't really understand the implications of that since we didn't have buses in Troy, it was clear to me that blacks were standing up for themselves and were supporting one another. The voice that I heard on the radio that day was Ralph David Abernathy, one of their leaders.

Ralph David Abernathy had been in Montgomery for a few years by the time Martin Luther King, Jr. arrived in the city. In 1952, while Martin was a doctoral student of theology at Boston University, Ralph, at 26 years of age, was called as senior pastor at the First Baptist Church, one of the largest black churches in the city. He and his church supported charitable efforts in the city, and so he became known in both the black and white communities. In 1954, the Dexter Avenue Baptist Church called Martin, at the age of twenty-five, to become their pastor. Dexter Avenue Baptist Church is just a "stone's throw" from the state capitol. When Martin was in the pulpit on Sunday mornings, he could see the front door of the capitol.

The two men came from different backgrounds. Martin grew up in a middle class family in Atlanta, the largest southern city. Ralph grew up on a farm in the Black Belt of Alabama. Because he lived in Atlanta, a city with many black professionals, Martin in some ways was sheltered from the hardcore racism in much of the rest of the South. On the other hand, Ralph had been faced with it every day. He couldn't go to a grocery store, or any place else, without seeing how black people were treated. The two men's upbringing was different as well. Martin grew up in a home that encouraged reading and getting an education and it was clear, early in Martin's life, that he was an intelligent young man. He, in fact, entered Morehouse College at the age of fifteen. Ralph, on the other hand, escaped life on the farm by serving in the military during World War II. After his tour of duty, he returned to Alabama, where he attended Alabama State College, a black college not academically up to the standards of Tuskegee or Morehouse.

Even though their backgrounds were different, they became lifelong friends and partners. Their differences complemented each other. Martin was the intellectual. Ralph was the "folksy" one who loved to engage people. They became friends as two young pastors, with wives from the same hometown. Coretta King and Juanita Abernathy were both from the town of Marion, Alabama, in Perry County. Martin and Ralph became partners when they formed the Montgomery Improvement Association and began the Montgomery Bus Boycott in December 1955. They led this boycott for more than a year until the U. S. Supreme Court struck down Alabama's bus segregation laws in December 1956. These two young men, pastors at two of the largest black churches in Montgomery, became partners in this effort and ultimately partners in a larger movement. But because they were the leaders and were seen by everyone, they became targets of the establishment and the hate groups. They paid the price for standing up for justice.

About a month after the bus boycott began, I heard on the radio that Dr. King's home had been bombed while he was giving a speech at Dr. Abernathy's church. Coretta, Juanita Abernathy, and the King's baby daughter, Yolanda, were in the King home, but fortunately escaped without injury. With the ever-present violence that threatened both of their families, Coretta and Juanita shared a common bond and were a great support to each other. At the end of the bus boycott, shortly after New Year's Day in 1957, Ralph's home and his church were bombed. He had been in Atlanta that night, with Martin and Coretta, planting the seed for a new national organization. Juanita and their baby were at home when the bomb exploded, but fortunately were not injured. The church, however, suffered extensive damage and had to be rebuilt. Four other black churches were bombed that night as well.

As the boycott continued, people around the nation saw on television what was happening in Montgomery. They saw people walking the streets of the city instead of riding on the buses, paying a heavy price for their cause. They also saw a young black preacher whose powerful voice and message of non-violence began to reverberate beyond Montgomery to the rest of the country. The people of Montgomery had never heard anyone like Dr. King before. An intellectual with the gift of eloquence, he quoted philosophers and theologians that the people had never heard of. Dr. King stood out in many ways to the people of Montgomery, including the white community which had never before faced a black man with credentials like his.

As he became better known, many opportunities began to come his way. He was sought after the boycott as a speaker around the country. He was offered book deals. He was no longer just a preacher and the pastor of Dexter Avenue Baptist Church in Montgomery. The world was beginning to open up for him, and now there were other ways for him to earn an income.

This was not the case for Ralph. His church was important to him, and he had taken out large loans to rebuild the church after the bombing.

Ralph was known as a good preacher and pastor, but the opportunities that Martin had to earn outside income were not as available to him. His pastoral position at First Baptist Church and his teaching position at Alabama State University were important to him and Juanita.

Martin Luther King, Sr.–"Daddy" King, as he was known to those of us in the Movement–was pastor of Ebenezer Baptist Church in Atlanta, and he wanted Martin to come back to Atlanta. He knew of the violence and the hatred in Alabama, and he felt that Atlanta would be safer for Martin and would be a better place for him to establish himself. When Martin's home was bombed, Daddy King was convinced that he was right. And then when Ralph's home was bombed, there was no doubt in his mind. Finally in 1960, Martin moved back to Atlanta and became co-pastor with his father at Ebenezer Baptist Church.

Martin and Ralph had planted the seed for the Southern Christian Leadership Conference after the Montgomery Bus Boycott had ended. Because of their success in Montgomery, people in other Southern cities began to call upon them for assistance in their struggle. Martin and Ralph soon realized they needed another organization that could respond to the calls they were receiving. They wanted an organization with non-violence and non-violent resistance as its primary focus. They decided it should be in Atlanta, just a few blocks from Ebenezer Baptist Church and from Martin's boyhood home.

When Martin left Montgomery, he knew that he wanted his partner in Atlanta with him. But Ralph felt that it wasn't necessary for him to live in Atlanta, that he could go from Montgomery to Atlanta for SCLC meetings or whenever he was needed. Martin needed to do some persuading in order to get Ralph to give up his church. If Ralph was to relocate to Atlanta, he would need to have a way to support his family. So Martin put out some feelers in the community to find a pastorate for Ralph in Atlanta, and through his efforts, Ralph was called to the West Hunter Street Baptist Church. In 1961, he finally joined Martin in Atlanta. Together they began to make SCLC the premier civil rights organization that it soon became.

I witnessed as a young boy what these two men had done in Montgomery. These two men were giants, "heroes" in my eyes. I had watched them, heard them, and wished that I was old enough to be with them. I had never dreamed that it would ever happen. But now, four years after Ralph had left Montgomery for Atlanta, I too had left Alabama for

Atlanta. I was now a part of this organization that Martin and Ralph had built. I stood in the middle of the floor at SCLC headquarters, wondering what would be next. What would their next project be? Where would they lead me? No longer did I have to witness it from afar. Now I was going to be a soldier in the fight. I was going to follow them wherever they led, walking in their footsteps, or walking arm in arm, shoulder to shoulder with them.

Getting Ready for the Fight

Now that I was officially a staff member, I was assigned to the field staff in the Voter Registration and Political Education Unit under the direction of Hosea Williams. Hosea, a chemist from Savannah, had been in charge of the summer's southern-wide voter registration (SCOPE) effort, which was now coming to an end. He was a courageous man, who knew how to organize and motivate people. He was emotional, but was able to think logically, perhaps because of his science background. Hosea was fearless when it came to confronting the power structure. A few months earlier in Selma, he had led the march on the Edmund Pettus Bridge that became known as Bloody Sunday when police brutally beat the marchers. That was just one of the many instances where Hosea showed his courage. During his years with SCLC, he went to jail more than anyone.

Hosea's office was located in a house that had been Dr. King's family home when he was growing up. It was now known as the SCOPE house, because Hosea had taken over the first floor and set up offices where he directed the campaign. There were bedrooms on the second and third floors for the use of SCLC staff. After my assignment to Hosea's unit, I went over to the SCOPE house to meet him. When I arrived, Hosea was not in the office, but Terrie Randolph, his administrative assistant, was. Terrie, who is white, had come to SCLC from the Midwest. She was a loyal person and was wonderful to work with. Except for a short stint as Ralph's assistant, Terrie was Hosea's right hand from the time she arrived until he died. She stayed with him even after he left SCLC and formed his own organization in Atlanta.

The other person in the office was Stoney Cooks, also an assistant to Hosea. Stoney, who was from the Northeast, was very intelligent and enjoyed getting into debates with other members of the staff. Years later he became the Executive Director of SCLC for a short period after Andy Young left to enter the political arena. He went on to work with Andy as his congressional chief of staff. Stoney was later appointed Deputy Ambassador to the UN when Andy became the UN Ambassador.

Terrie told me to get my stuff from the YMCA and move into one of the bedrooms upstairs. She explained that she would give me a per diem check so I would have money to take care of the personal things that I needed, such as food and clothes. This was my first paycheck from SCLC. I shared a room with two or three other staff people. One was Lester, "Big Lester," Hankerson, who had come from Savannah with Hosea.

Later that day I finally met Hosea, who welcomed me on board. We talked about what I would be doing and where I might work. I said that I had met with Dr. King and told him that Dr. King wanted me to commit myself to non-violence before I actually went into the field. I had already started reading about Gandhi, his movement in India, and how he used non-violence to change an entire nation. I was beginning to learn something about the philosophy behind non-violence, and I was learning about the tactics that Gandhi had used in that country. It was becoming clearer to me why Dr. King emphasized non-violence, which he had done right from the very beginning when the Montgomery Bus Boycott began in 1955.

Hosea outlined the training that I would have to undergo. I would need to learn how to act when I was confronted by racists or police, and how to protect myself if I were beaten. But I also needed to know how to protect others in my midst, how to lead demonstrations, how to maintain control of a crowd and not allow them to get out of hand, how to make sure that outside people did not break into a march, and how to confront police, especially when we were committing civil disobedience. I would be taught about the different kinds of tactics used and how to train people on the local level about demonstrations and discipline. I would learn about government and how it functions, as well as how to teach this kind of information to people on the local level.

After my meeting with Hosea, I continued to work out of the office of the Citizenship Education Program for a couple weeks before going to the Penn Center for the training. I hadn't been able to talk with Leon for some time about all of the changes taking place in my life. While I had been at the Penn Center, Leon had closed up the office in Troy and driven to Atlanta to submit his report and pick up "Princess," his cocker spaniel, who had spent the summer with SCLC staff at the SCOPE house. By the time I got to Atlanta, he and Princess were on their way back to New Rochelle. Once he arrived, I was finally able to tell him what was happening–the amazing events that he had set in motion by recommending me for the SCLC training at the Penn Center.

Finally, it was time to return to the Penn Center to undergo the training outlined to me by Dr. King and Hosea. Several of us left the SCLC office in a caravan of cars and vans and headed to St. Helena Island. Other SCLC staff members, both new and old, were also arriving at the Penn Center from around the South. There were also people from other organizations and groups that had been working with SCLC.

Dr. King came for a day and outlined the precepts of non-violence for the group. During my two weeks in Atlanta, I had seen Dr. King in the office from time to time, spoken to him, and on a few occasions engaged in small talk with him. Soon after I arrived in Atlanta, I had gone to his church on a Sunday and heard him deliver the sermon, so this was the second time that I had heard him speak. But this time he was in a hall at the Penn Center, and I was sitting two rows from him. It seemed that he was speaking just to me. I sat there, feeding on his every word, learning about the philosophy of non-violence from him, and committing myself to what he expected of me and all of the staff of SCLC.

On a personal level I had to work at keeping my cool. I had a tendency to lose my temper if I felt that someone was abusing me, either verbally or physically, and I would react with anger. The training included role-playing in situations where people were being abusive and violent. This was difficult for me, but I was willing to endure it for the sake of Dr. King and the Movement. This was not about me. It was about the lives of people I would be leading.

Usually, James Bevel or his wife Diane Nash would lead this portion of the training, although occasionally Andy Young took the lead. We used both indoors and outdoors for the role-playing. Inside the hall, a

public facility, such as a restaurant, where you might be attacked would
be simulated. You might be sitting at a table, and then the chair would be
kicked out from under you and someone would drag you across the floor.
Or you could be sitting on a stool at a counter and someone would grab
you by the collar from behind, which is what James Bevel did to me during
the first session. This kind of training would pay off for me during my time
in the Movement, because I would have these kinds of experiences.

We used the outdoors to simulate marches and civil disobedience. Even
though I had been volunteering in Troy and had led several demonstrations,
I had not been taught until then about tactics and strategy. We would
role-play different scenarios and how we would act if confronted by the
police–whether we would go willingly if arrested or whether we would
resist and have to be carried off. We learned how to protect ourselves if we
were beaten by the police. I realized that this training could save my life
and that of my co-workers, as well as the lives of people I would be working
with when I was assigned to a community.

I came to understand during this training how important non-
violence was to the Movement. If we were going to mobilize hundreds and
thousands of people, we had to do it in a non-violent way. Even though,
in some instances, we were going to be committing civil disobedience, we
still needed to be peaceful and non-violent. We couldn't allow hundreds
of people to violently go up against police and sheriffs.

At some of the other training sessions, I learned more about SCLC
itself and how it operated. I learned about the connection between the
national SCLC and its affiliate organizations, such as the Alabama
Christian Leadership Conference, in several southern states. I began to
gain more knowledge of how government works. It was necessary that
we be knowledgeable about major issues, such as voter registration, and
how the laws relating to a particular issue work. For example, we needed
to know all about HUD, the U.S. Department of Housing and Urban
Development, when we were dealing with the issue of fair housing. We
needed to know what laws were in place and how to use them to our
advantage. I learned later that doing this was so important that before we
went into any major campaign, we would have a retreat to discuss the issues
in depth. If we were going to organize people, we needed to understand the
issues thoroughly in order to know what to request, or demand, from the
government and pass this information along to people at the local level.

The training at the Penn Center also provided an opportunity for me to get to know people, both within SCLC and outside. It was important to get to know co-workers and colleagues, especially the field staff that I would be working with in different communities. Since you had to rely on these people, you needed to know how they would react in situations. One of the people that I got to know and worked closely with for most of my time with SCLC was James Orange, a young man from Birmingham, who was only a couple years older than me. James had been recommended to Dr. King and then hired by him, as I had been.

Another person that I met at the Penn Center was Lynn Gilroy, a white woman from California who worked for the American Friends Society. Lynn had been down south working with people in various communities on a grass roots level and had come to the Penn Center for some training. I was fairly shy and unsophisticated, and I had never had any kind of relationship with someone like Lynn, since it had been drilled into me since I was a child to avoid white women. This was the reason that I had not become friends with Elizabeth Shamburger back in Troy a couple months before. And yet here at the Penn Center, where the interaction between blacks and whites was so different from what I was accustomed to, I became comfortable enough to become friends with Lynn. I even found myself hoping it might develop into something more. We did in fact go out together a couple times after we had both returned to Atlanta, although I was uneasy being in public with her. But Atlanta is a large city, different from most Southern cities and much more sophisticated. Relationships between whites and blacks were easier there than in other parts of the South. Spending time with Lynn helped me with my shyness, and I began to be more comfortable with women in general. Soon, however, we went our separate ways.

After the training at the Penn Center was over, I was anxious to get my first assignment as an SCLC staff member. But I was disappointed to find that I had been assigned to go back to Troy to monitor the voter registration that we had begun early that summer and recruit some people who might be willing to go through the Citizenship Training. Hosea often made this kind of assignment in order for people to follow-up on a project they had been involved in.

I didn't want to go back to Troy for a number of reasons. I wanted to move forward and work in a different community. And I still had some of the same concerns that I had during the SCOPE project–that my family could experience repercussions from my work. There was also the fact of the broken relationship with my father. Although I wasn't happy when Hosea suggested that I go back to Troy, I understood his reasoning. I also knew that there was going to be a major push for voter registration in the Black Belt of Alabama, so I hoped I wouldn't be in Troy for long.

When I arrived in Troy, I went first to meet with Johnnie Mae Warren. In addition to getting updated on what was going on in Troy, I arranged with her to stay at the old freedom house while I was in town. I then met with other leaders to assess what had been taking place. I was particularly interested in how the integrated group had been working, whether it was doing the kind of things that we had hoped for. I was pleased to learn that they had had several meetings and had begun some promising work. I also conducted several workshops with community leaders and others; these workshops were based on the training I had received from Septima Clark during my first visit to the Penn Center.

During the short time I was in Troy, I was able to spend some time with my mother and some of my cousins, but I had no real encounter with my father, aside from seeing him on the sidewalk across the street one morning. I also met with Judge Reeves and was pleased to see that the local power structure still assumed that I was an outsider working with SCLC. The assignment back in Troy lasted about a month, and then I got a call from Albert Turner, the field secretary for SCLC in Alabama, who told me that I had been reassigned to Selma.

Selma

I hadn't been back to Selma since the day that Leon had driven me there to catch the bus to the Penn Center. This time crossing the Edmund Pettus Bridge heading into Selma, I knew more about the events around Bloody Sunday and had met some of the people who marched that day. SNCC (Student Nonviolent Coordinating Committee) and SCLC had been working in Selma on a voter registration campaign for a couple of years. Since Dallas County had a black population of more than 60 percent, it could mean a significant political shift if they were registered to vote. With their votes, badly needed changes could be made in Selma and throughout Dallas County. In January and February 1965, as part of this campaign, SCLC led a series of demonstrations.

On February 17 in nearby Marion, Jimmie Lee Jackson was shot and killed by an Alabama state trooper while participating in a peaceful march from his church to the Perry County jail where SCLC staff member James Orange was being held. In response to this incident, SCLC planned a march from Selma to Montgomery on March 7. Hosea Williams, representing SCLC, and John Lewis, representing SNCC, led several hundred people towards the bridge as they began their march, but they were met by police who would not let them advance across the bridge. The marchers were severely beaten by police with night sticks and cattle prods and were trampled by horses. John Lewis was beaten unconscious.

The conscience of America was awakened by the shocking images of

Bloody Sunday that appeared on television news programs. People came to Selma from around the country to lend support, and tragically, two of them would soon be killed. Immediately after Bloody Sunday, Dr. King had sent out a message for religious leaders to join him in Selma for a second march. Some 450 religious leaders from around the country came to Selma for this second attempt to cross the Edmund Pettus Bridge. They were joined by 200 local blacks, and on March 9 they marched across the bridge. The marchers were turned back by police, but this time there was no violence. The violence came later that night when Jim Reeb, a Unitarian Universalist minister from Boston, was beaten to death as he left a restaurant in downtown Selma.

Finally, later that month, the third attempt to march from Selma to Montgomery was successful. President Lyndon Johnson had federalized the Alabama National Guard to insure that the marchers would be protected. The fifty-mile march, led by Dr. King and Dr. Abernathy, took almost a week to complete. So that there would not be overwhelming numbers of people on the road at one time, a limited number of people marched the entire fifty miles to Montgomery. People joined the march at different points along the route and then dropped out. Both Mrs. King and Mrs. Abernathy walked part of the way. The number of people marching increased, however, as the march got closer to Montgomery. On March 25, the march concluded on the steps of the Alabama State Capitol, and Dr. King spoke to the nearly 25,000 people there. It was that night on her way back to Selma that Viola Liuzzo, a housewife from Michigan, was shot to death on Highway 80.

A few days later President Johnson spoke to a joint session of Congress and introduced the Voting Rights legislation. Johnson concluded his speech with the words, "We shall overcome." I hadn't heard that phrase used by anyone other than those of us in the Movement. Hearing those words from the President was a powerful moment for us. The Voting Rights Act was passed in August 1965. I was assigned to Selma a month or so after that landmark legislation.

When I arrived in Selma and reported to the SCLC office, I was told that they hadn't yet found a place for me to stay, but were working on it. They suggested that while I was waiting, I walk over to Brown Chapel AME Church, where most of the staff members were conducting workshops. Brown Chapel is one of the largest black churches in Selma and is close to downtown, two reasons that it had became headquarters for the Movement in Selma. I went over to the church and watched what the staff were doing, knowing that I would be conducting workshops myself while I was in Selma.

After a while, one of the staff invited me to go with him to the home of the West family, who lived in the housing project behind Brown Chapel. The Wests had been very involved since the early stages of the campaign. Because they lived so close to Brown Chapel, those of us in the Movement from out of town spent a lot of time at their house. Even though they were poor, the Wests opened their home to all of us, feeding us and sharing what little they had. I would soon find that, after spending the day out in the rural areas, I would return to town and go to the West's home and crash on their floor to get some rest. The Wests had several children, and all were involved in what we were doing.

But two of the girls, about five and six years old, became a symbol of the campaign. Hosea and Dr. King would occasionally take the girls on marches. These two little girls stood out because of their young age and their beautiful smiles, and they symbolized the future. If we were able to get their parents and others like them to register to vote and hopefully bring about change in Selma, these young children would have a better life when they reached adulthood. The Wests were representative of the majority of blacks in Selma and Dallas County. They were poor and had migrated from a farm to the city. Selma and Dallas County may have had a larger black professional class than Troy and Pike County, but nevertheless the county as a whole was quite poor.

One of the people I met at the West home that first day was Leroy Moton, a local boy a little younger than me. Leroy had been in the car with Viola Liuzzo the night she was killed, and he had been shot as well. Leroy described to me the horror of that night, the night that this young mother gave her life to support the black people of Alabama in their effort to gain the right to vote. I was completely stunned, and it was then that I truly realized the danger of what I was doing. It was the first time that I took seriously the possibility that my life might be taken. Even though I had told Dr. King in all honesty that I was willing to give my life for the Movement, the possibility of that happening had been theoretical. But as I listened to Leroy and saw his wounds, it suddenly became real to me. I realized that what had happened to him could happen to me. When I later visited the scene where Reverend Reeb had given his life, I was more determined than ever to serve. I was willing to make whatever sacrifice had to be made, as they had done.

This was a reaffirmation for me of that moment when I first stood up in Troy and spoke at a mass meeting and realized that I was involved in something much larger than myself. I was willing to follow Dr. King and Dr. Abernathy wherever they led. I knew it would not be easy in Selma and Dallas County; this was obvious from everything that had happened. I knew of the reputation of Sheriff Jim Clark and Police Chief Wilson Baker.

We went out to the plantations and tried to convince the black folks who worked on them to go to the courthouse and register to vote. This was dangerous for us and for them, because we never knew when we might run into the plantation owner. We didn't know what his reaction would be to us and how that reaction might affect the black people living on the plantation. Some of these black people seldom left the plantation, except to go to the doctor. Trying to persuade them to go to the courthouse in town was difficult, but eventually they started to come. These were courageous people. They lived in isolated rural areas or in very small towns. Anything could happen to them, and no one would know. I understood their situation from my own experience living on a plantation.

Even though we brought people in from the rural areas, most did not get registered. The registrars in Dallas County were using tactics similar to those used in my hometown. Even though the Voting Rights Act had passed by then, the registrars were still charging poll tax and slowing the process down to discourage people from turning out. Unlike what we were able to accomplish in Troy, the registrars outright refused to see people except on the designated day.

The workshops conducted by staff prepared people to march on the courthouse and be arrested. Jim Clark had shown his hand on Bloody Sunday, so we all knew what he was capable of doing. Mass meetings at Brown Chapel or one of the other black churches were almost a nightly occurrence. Usually, they took place in Selma, but some were held in other parts of Dallas County. Occasionally, we would have two mass meetings in the same neighborhood. This was particularly true when Dr. King or Dr. Abernathy were in town and planned to speak. So many people would turn out to hear them that we needed the extra space. At times, other national figures would come to Selma to speak.

But the speakers at most of the mass meetings in Selma were Hosea Williams, James Bevel, or Andy Young. Hosea was a good singer and would often get people energized by singing. Freedom songs were important during the Movement. They helped to motivate and inspire us as we went into battle. One of Hosea's favorite freedom songs was "Keep Your Eyes on the Prize." The lyrics read in part, "I know one thing that we did right was the day we started to fight. Keep your eyes on the prize. Hold on. Hold on." This freedom song was based on an old slave spiritual: "Keep your hand on the plow, hold on…" I would sit there listening to Hosea, remembering how my grandmother used to walk the floors of our house singing that spiritual.

The mass meetings were intended to motivate and educate the people of Dallas County. When the meetings were held outside of Selma, the speaker would usually be someone like James Orange or me. I spoke on a number of occasions in Dallas County. We would also conduct workshops at Brown Chapel to prepare people for the marches. Staff alternated their duties between reaching out to people, educating them, bringing them to the courthouse, and direct action, such as leading marches.

We began to march on the courthouse almost daily to show that blacks were ready and willing to vote, and we continued to apply this pressure. We sometimes marched two or three times a day. We would march in the morning and again in the afternoon, trying to reach the courthouse and gain entrance into it. But in most of our attempts, we would be beaten back by Jim Clark and his deputies, or thrown in jail. Many people were injured and many arrested, myself included. On one occasion Jim Clark himself stung me with an electric cattle prod while I was leading a march on the courthouse. He and his deputies were there every day to stop us before we reached the courthouse.

Someone, perhaps James Bevel, came up with the idea of having a march of elementary school children. Hosea and Andy led this march along with Yolanda King, who was ten at the time. This is the first time that I remember Yolanda being involved in direct action. Thankfully, the march was completed with no violence.

We were in communication with the Justice Department while all of this was going on, reporting that hundreds and thousands of people were being turned away and that we continued to face the hostility of Sheriff Jim Clark's forces. Sheriff Clark was a man who was easily riled and reacted with force even though he knew the Justice Department was watching his actions. Many black people were arrested and beaten by Sheriff Clark's forces, but nevertheless, they continued to come in significant numbers.

Through SCLC's efforts, we were able to demonstrate to the Justice Department the need for federal registrars, not only for Dallas County but for the entire Black Belt of Alabama. The "Black Belt" is an area of Alabama with black soil, but it also is the region where blacks are in the majority. The Black Belt consists of Dallas County, Perry County, Hale County, Greene County, and a few others. When the federal registrars arrived in Dallas County, they set up shop in the basement of the post office. Since the post office is a federal facility, the registrars could by-pass local officials, and Sheriff Clark would not be able to interrupt the process. A number of FBI agents were there to insure the safety of the federal registrars as well as those registering to vote. We brought in large numbers of people, and hundreds were being registered each day. The federal registrars soon determined that they needed more registrars and additional facilities to accommodate all the people who were coming. In some communities the post offices were too small to use for voter registration. If there were no other federal facilities, the federal registrars brought in trailers or rented halls.

One of the SCLC staff who had helped train me was Diane Nash. This was her second time in Selma, as it was for some of the others. Diane was a veteran of the lunch counter sit-in's and the freedom rides, and she had played an instrumental role in the Birmingham campaign in 1963. She was very intelligent and was an excellent strategist and tactician. A beautiful, light-skinned woman, she was married to James Bevel, and they were an awesome team for SCLC. I admired Diane's intellect and her courage, as well as her ability to motivate and move people. Diane was the only woman who worked in the field for SCLC. From time to time some women were brought in from the national office to work on projects, but they primarily served in supporting roles, whereas Diane was on the front lines, organizing people and leading demonstrations.

On a local level women were often leaders in their community, but on a national level women were not given leadership roles and were not respected for their gifts and talent. SNCC had more women in the field than SCLC, but even they had only one woman in a position of authority at that time–Kathleen Cleaver, who became better known years later as one of the leaders of the Black Panther Party. In spite of the lack of opportunities for women in the Movement, they were extremely important. Without women, like the mothers who came out and marched and supported their children, the Movement most likely would not have been the success that it was.

It was in Selma that I first met a number of national celebrities. Harry Belafonte, Sammy Davis Jr., and Gregory Peck all came to support what we were doing. But it was Joan Baez and Harry Belafonte that I came to know best. Harry Belafonte was a staunch supporter of Dr. King and SCLC, and he, like Joan, would spend time with Dr. King and the staff, particularly at retreats. Joan Baez did this as well, but she also came to other places where SCLC was working. She came to perform, but also to work with women and children. During the time in Selma, I was often asked to pick her up from the airport, which was fifty miles away in Montgomery. Joan also attended SCLC's staff retreats and performed for the staff there, helping us to relax. After I got to know her, she would usually ask if I might be available to pick her up at an airport. If I was in the area, I was always glad to do this and spend some time with her.

When staff was assigned to communities, we would try to find homes where we could stay, rather than staying in hotels. In fact, many communities had no black-owned hotels, although this was not the case in Selma. But by staying in homes in the black community, we could be close to the people we were working with. The people of Selma opened up their homes to us, and I stayed with several families during my time there. I spent two or three weeks in the home of Amelia Boynton, a businesswoman and a leader of the Dallas County Voting League, the group that had invited SCLC to Selma. She recently turned 100 years old. I moved from her home to a freedom house when space was available.

Sometimes if a significant number of staff was in a community and a house was available, a "freedom house" would be set up. There was a large number of SCLC and SNCC staff in Selma. So in Selma, the freedom house was established for both SCLC and SNCC staff to live together. Several years before, SCLC had created the Student Nonviolent Coordinating Committee (SNCC) as a way to involve college students in the Movement. Although the organizations were now separate, they often worked closely together.

However, from time to time, conflicts arose between the two groups. The conflicts usually concerned who got paid the most, who worked the hardest, and who was willing to take on the more dangerous areas. None of us in the Movement was paid very much, just enough to survive. But those of us with SCLC were paid more than the SNCC staff, who were not paid a great deal, so there was some jealousy on the part of the SNCC staff. Some SCLC staff, including myself, went into Lowndes County and worked in the county, but usually we would return to Selma by night. It was the SNCC staff who did most of the work in Lowndes County. They were really the ones who worked to get the people of Lowndes County registered to vote and who educated them politically.

SNCC staff felt that SCLC staff was afraid to be in Lowndes County, and in some ways SNCC was right. We didn't really want to work in Lowndes County because of its long history of brutality and violence; Viola Liuzzo had been killed there only a few months before. The SCLC staff was always worried about the safety of Dr. King and Dr. Abernathy. They were out front in our campaigns and their lives were constantly being threatened. We felt that Lowndes County was too dangerous for them to spend any length of time. We knew that we couldn't count on sheriffs like Jim Clark to protect them. But truthfully, we were also concerned about our own lives. The SNCC staff was mostly college students, whereas the SCLC staff tended to be older and included a lot of ministers.

While I was in Selma, Jonathan Daniels, an Episcopal seminarian from New Hampshire, was killed in Lowndes County. Daniels had gone from Selma to participate in a demonstration in Lowndes County. He and several others were arrested at the demonstration and taken to jail. They were let out of jail but were confronted down the street by a special deputy, who aimed his gun at a sixteen-year old black girl in the group. Daniels was shot and killed as he pushed the girl to the ground to save her from the shotgun blast. Richard Morrisroe, a priest, was also shot but survived.

Sadly, the killers were all acquitted in the murders of the three people who had come to Alabama to support our struggle that year. The Klansmen who shot down Viola Liuzzo were acquitted. The men who beat Jim Reeb to death were acquitted. The deputy who killed Jonathan Daniels was acquitted. These three incidents reaffirmed for me that my life could be taken away at any moment. It was here in Selma that I realized what Dr. King had to deal with every day. And as I continued with my part in the fight for freedom, I appreciated even more the courage and dedication of Dr. King.

From time to time, someone would donate an old car to SCLC, which would then be assigned to a member of the SCLC staff. I had the use of one of these old cars, which unfortunately had an accelerator that would sometimes stick, making it difficult to stop the car. One day I was asked to go to Barber County to pick up a staff member, a young white woman, and bring her back to Selma. Another male staff member came with me so I wouldn't be driving alone at night. We had to go through Lowndes County in order to return to Selma, and the fact that Mrs. Liuzzo, who was white, had been killed in Lowndes County was very high on my radar. After we had picked up the woman, as we approached Lowndes County, we stopped on the side of the road and asked her to get into the trunk. We felt that it would be dangerous for all of us if two black men were seen riding with a white woman late at night. We all breathed a sigh of relief when we made it through Lowndes County safely without being stopped by the sheriff or a policeman.

But as we got closer to Selma, the accelerator chose that moment to stick. My colleague got down on the floor and tried unsuccessfully to release the gas pedal. Here we went, speeding down the road, unable to stop the car, with a white woman in the trunk! I was afraid that if we were spotted by the Dallas County Sheriff's Department in a speeding car, they would think we were trying to flee from them. And if they found the woman in the trunk, at the very least we might be charged with kidnapping. But luckily, just as we were approaching the Edmund Pettus Bridge on the edge of downtown Selma, my colleague was finally able to fix the accelerator and we arrived back at Brown Chapel safely. All three of us were shaken by our experience and were thankful to be safe and secure back in the black community. This was one of the few incidents where I had been really afraid. I was so afraid that I prayed out loud, asking God to stop the runaway car. Most of the time I took whatever was happening in stride—at least outwardly. But on this occasion, I was truly afraid.

This was the time of Woodstock, and some of the staff decided to go from Selma to Woodstock. I considered going as well, because I knew that

Joan Baez would be performing, but I finally decided not to go with them. Instead, I went home to Troy to visit my family for a few days.

As a young boy, I had often walked the six or seven miles to town from our home. On this visit, I started walking from town to my mother's house. I had almost made it home when I was picked up by the FBI and taken back to town where they brought me to the police station to interrogate me. The FBI was interested in learning more about Stokely Carmichael. Stokely was one of the SNCC staff members who lived in the freedom house with me. He was moving up in the organization and, although I didn't know it at the time, he would soon become Chairman of SNCC, replacing John Lewis. The FBI assumed, because we lived in the freedom house together, that I would have information about him. I refused to answer any of their questions, and in fact knew very little about Stokely's activities besides the fact that he was the project director for SNCC in Lowndes County. They questioned me for a couple hours and then drove me to my mother's house in the country.

There were many FBI agents in Selma. I came to know a few of them, particularly the agents from the North. I saw a difference in the agents from outside of Alabama, as opposed to those from Alabama. Those from Alabama tended to have a relationship with the police or sheriff's departments, and I sometimes wondered whether some of them provided information on us to those departments. It was on this brief visit home to Troy that I realized for the first time that I was being watched by the FBI. This surveillance was not to protect me, but to get information about my activities. They obviously had a file on me. They knew where I was staying back in Selma and who some of the other people were in the freedom house. They knew I had gone to Troy and where to find me.

Now I realized I had something else to worry about. Not only did I have to be concerned about angry whites, Klansmen, and vicious policemen, but I had to be concerned about the FBI as well and what they were up to. As far as I knew, no one was aware that I had been picked up by the FBI and questioned, except those police officers on duty when the FBI brought me in to the Troy police station. I didn't tell my family about it, because they would have worried. It certainly wouldn't have helped mend my relationship with my father, which was broken already because of my activities in the Movement.

After a few days, I returned to Selma. After hearing about the conditions in Woodstock, I was glad that I had made the decision not to go. Too many people had gathered in this one spot in New York, and it had rained often. On the other hand, if I had gone, the crowded, muddy festival would have better prepared me for Resurrection City in Washington, DC, a couple years later.

Even though I was still officially assigned to Selma and Dallas County, I began to work in some of the other nearby counties in Alabama on voter registration, and I occasionally participated in demonstrations. This was the beginning of my move from Selma into other potentially dangerous places. Many other sheriffs in the Black Belt of Alabama were like Jim Clark and were willing to find any excuse to beat and jail you. I knew how much blood had been shed in Selma and how many had given their lives to register people. As I started working in other places, I wondered how much more blood would be shed. Who would be next? Would it be me? Or would it be someone I had grown to care about? How many more churches would be burned or bombed? But I knew that the fight had to go on, even if it meant more bloodshed, more lives lost.

Greene County, Alabama

As we began to see some success in registering people in Dallas County in late 1965 and early 1966, SCLC decided to concentrate on registering as many people as possible in the rest of the Black Belt of Alabama. Staff were reassigned to all of the counties in that part of the state. I was doing some work in Perry County even while still assigned to Selma. Then in early 1966, along with some other staff members, I was assigned to Greene County.

Rev. Thomas Gilmore, who was originally from Greene County, was the project leader. After living for a short time in the North, he had returned to Eutaw, Alabama, a couple years before. For the past year, Gilmore had worked for SCLC in a couple of the more southern counties in Alabama. Once the decision was made to move into Greene County, he was the logical person to be the project director since Greene County was his home and he knew it better than anyone else on the SCLC staff. Gilmore, who pastored a small church in Eutaw, was a young, easy-going person and fun to be around. He was about five years older than me and already had a family. In spite of these differences, we had much in common and developed a good relationship–both personal and professional–and I would often spend time with him and his family. Gilmore's calling was first and foremost to the ministry, but he also had a calling to make life better for the people of Greene County. So like me, when SCLC came into the area, he took the opportunity to join them and fight the injustices he was witnessing.

In addition to dealing with brutal sheriffs and police chiefs in Greene County and other counties, we also had to deal with the knowledge that the Ku Klux Klan was running rampant and terrorizing black people. The people who lived in rural areas and on plantations were especially vulnerable and were a particular target. Nevertheless, we called upon those people to stand up. As in Dallas County, we marched on the courthouse and throughout the town of Eutaw, the county seat, in order to get people registered to vote.

Eutaw was still dealing with the issue of public accommodation. Even though the Civil Rights Act had been passed almost two years before, blacks were still being denied access to public accommodations, such as restaurants and hotels. We had a very diverse staff in Greene County, both in terms of race and gender, and one day we decided to go to lunch at one of the restaurants that was refusing to serve blacks. There were about five of us, two white women, one white man, and two black men. We placed our orders and since they realized we were "outsiders," they decided to serve us. While we were waiting, I was stabbed in the back with a pointed stick or some sharp object. I had my back to the door and was unable to see who had approached from the rear. The police came and once the situation quieted down, a local person who supported us took me to the emergency room in Tuscaloosa, about ten miles away in the next county since there was no hospital in Eutaw. Even though my wound was not serious, this incident has stayed with me through the years, and I am still uncomfortable sitting with my back to the door in a restaurant. The physical scars heal, but the psychological scars linger.

In Eutaw we marched almost every day, and sometimes we would march at night. Mostly, we would try to march on the courthouse because that is where people had to go to register to vote. But on occasion we would march in the white neighborhoods. Greene County and Eutaw were like most cities and towns in Alabama, with a distinct separation of black and white neighborhoods. Tom Gilmore or I led most of the marches and demonstrations. Although Gilmore was on the staff of SCLC, he was a local leader as well so he had a dual responsibility. I was second in command to him in his SCLC role, and accompanied by a local leader, we would alternate leading these demonstrations.

There were usually a couple hundred people marching with us. We deliberately kept the number lower than we could actually produce for two reasons. The same people would not have to march each time and could get some rest between marches. Also, if the sheriff or city police arrested us, there were less people that would have to be bailed out of jail and our financial resources would last longer. Occasionally, Albert Turner or Hosea Williams would come in and lead demonstrations of more than 500 people. On these occasions we wanted to show that we could produce larger numbers. The officials could see that if Dr. King himself came in to lead demonstrations, we could produce even larger numbers.

As we had done in other places in Alabama, on registration days we would bus people in from outlying areas. By this time, we were fairly good at getting people to come to the courthouse. As in Selma and Dallas County, federal registrars enabled us to register a great many people. The registrars were usually set up downstairs in the post office. But in some cases they would go out to some of the smaller towns because we were turning people out in such great numbers.

Two incidents occurred in Greene County that I remember well even today. One of the hazards of the Movement was that you were in constant battle. You moved from one battleground to the next. I have a tendency to hold things inside, and one of the results of this is that I developed a case of ulcers, serious enough that I had to be treated at a hospital in Atlanta. One evening we held a rally at one of the largest churches in Eutaw. Hosea Williams was the main speaker that evening, and he was going to lead a march of about 600 people the next morning. I went outside the church and was standing on the steps talking with several other staff people, when I had a severe ulcer attack and I bent over in pain. Almost simultaneously, either a car backfired or someone shot a gun nearby. When people standing near me saw me double over, they thought I had been shot and began to yell and move into the road. The other staff members and I tried to calm the situation by explaining what was happening with me. Keeping people under control when something unexpected occurred was one of the things we were trained to do. This incident illustrates how quickly a crowd can get out of control, and how, in a peaceful setting, a mob can form.

The other incident I remember as clearly as if it was yesterday. Stokely Carmichael and I were leading a march of about 250 people from the church, and we were headed downtown to the courthouse. The police department had come up with a new tactic to prevent us from getting to our destination, a tactic that Jim Clark in Selma had used fairly effectively.

They would let us leave the church and begin the march, but would stop us some distance from our destination. On this occasion, we were stopped by the police near a bridge leading into downtown and were ordered to turn around. I refused to turn around and insisted that we were going to march to the courthouse. Someone–either Thomas Gilmore or Rev. William Branch, a pastor and local leader–began to pray. After the prayer was over, I repeated to the police chief that we were going to march to the courthouse that day.

I was almost daring the police chief to arrest all of us or force us back to the church. I had been in the county jail a couple times already. The jail was an older facility with the radio dispatch in the jail itself, and at night as you lay in your cell, you could hear the radio calls. Impulsively, and probably foolishly, I told the police chief that they could either shoot me or let us go to the courthouse. I told them that if they shot me, I would still march. If they killed me, I would come back. I don't know if I was more courageous because I was standing beside Stokely or not, but at this point, Stokely began to move forward, and I moved with him. Stokely said, "Get out of our way," and the police let us through. Although law enforcement agencies knew about Stokely, he was not known by the general public at that time. But that would change a month or two later. This was one of the situations that made me realize how lucky, or blessed, I was throughout the years that I was a freedom fighter.

Our work in Greene County paid off a few years later. We were able to register a large percentage of the eligible black population, and we educated the community about their responsibility and rights as voters. Once we had registered people, we began to search for people who would step forward and run for political office. We did this not only in Greene County, but also throughout the Black Belt, and we were successful in recruiting people. Rev. William Branch ran for probate judge, and Thomas Gilmore himself ran for sheriff. The first time Gilmore lost by a narrow margin, but the second time, he won in a landslide. Eventually, blacks held almost all positions in Greene County, from commissioners to school board members. Greene County began the wave that would sweep across the Black Belt and beyond.

Gilmore was well liked throughout the county, and the fact that he was a member of the clergy added another dimension to what he brought to the position. Normally, sheriffs were tough, rugged guys or ex-military types, as opposed to someone who believed in non-violence and was a man of God. By choosing not to wear a gun, he gave the people of Greene County a new image of a sheriff. Someone who could be peaceful, rather than brutal. Someone who could talk and negotiate, rather than being violent. Several years later, a movie, *Sheriff without a Gun*, starring Lou Gossett, Jr. was made about Gilmore becoming the first black sheriff of Greene County, and it focused on his carrying SCLC's philosophy of non-violence into his new role. After his three terms, Gilmore went back to his first calling–the ministry–and relocated to Birmingham.

In later years, I arranged for Gilmore to come to Providence while we were trying to recruit blacks for the police department. I felt that he would be a good role model for young blacks. I had him speak at mass meetings that I held in the community, as well as to student groups at Brown University.

It often happened that people from other communities would see what was happening near them, and feel that they should do something in their communities as well. This had happened ever since the Montgomery Bus Boycott, when people saw what was happening in Montgomery and felt that they needed to stand up as well. That was one of the reasons SCLC came into being. When other communities started to request Martin's help, he and Ralph started an organization that could provide assistance.

While I was working in Greene County, black leaders from Pickens County came to Eutaw to see if SCLC could send some staff to assist them. The county, which had a population of just over 20,000, was northwest of Greene County. I was assigned to Pickens County with another staff member, Johnny Travis, to do an assessment of the problems there. Some time before, SNCC had had some staff in Pickens County, but they were not there very long.

Pickens County was a difficult place for blacks to live, and they were intimidated by the history of violence that had been inflicted upon them. One of the major legends in the county was that in 1878 a black man had been hung outside the courthouse, and that his image could still be seen in the courthouse window. I wanted to see this for myself, so when we arrived in Carrollton, the county seat, I went over to the courthouse. I discovered to my surprise that when I stood across from the courthouse, I could clearly see the image in the window upstairs. I didn't understand it, but whatever caused it, the image still served as a symbol of violence to black people almost a hundred years later.

As in most cases when we moved into a community, we hoped to stay in someone's home. When Johnny and I arrived, we were told that they had found someone willing for us to stay in their home. It was clear to us that they were somewhat concerned about our presence, but were courageous enough to welcome us. We were there only two or three days before the word got to the white community that some civil rights workers were in town. Soon the word began to circulate in the black community that the Klan was looking for us and that they would burn down the home of anyone that allowed us to stay. When word got to the family we were staying with that the Klan was going to come that night and burn their place down, they told us that we could not stay with them any longer and that we were not safe in Carrollton. No one else was willing to take us in so we decided to leave and go back to Greene County. Even then, the fear in the black community was so strong that no one would give us a ride. The violence that had been inflicted upon this community over the years was very much a part of the people's consciousness.

Knowing that the Klan was looking for us, Johnny and I desperately tried to find a way back to Greene County. But with no one willing to help us, the only way for us to make it out was on foot. We literally ran through fields as we escaped, since it was too dangerous for us to be on the road where we could easily be picked up and killed. We were able to get out of town this way, and when we got closer to Greene County, we stopped at the home of a black family. When we told them of our situation, one of the family members drove us the rest of the way.

Unfortunately, the black leaders from Pickens County hadn't done a real assessment. They knew what the problems were, but they hadn't determined whether the people were ready for a movement, whether they were ready to take the kind of action and suffer the consequences, as the people of Greene County were doing. As we discovered, the people were not ready. They were not ready when SNCC had gone in earlier. The fear and intimidation that had existed the past hundred years was still a factor. The fact that they were unable to even drive us out of the county proved to me that a movement in Pickens County was a long way off. I was not willing to go back to Pickens County and put my life on the line, knowing that there would be little support from the black community. In fact, I haven't been back to Pickens County since that time, even though I have revisited most of the other places that I worked.

The Meredith March

After my escape from Pickens County, I submitted my report to SCLC and resumed my work in Greene County. I wasn't back in Greene County for too long before rumors began to spread that James Meredith was planning to walk across Mississippi. He had decided that he was going to walk to the state capital in Jackson, Mississippi. He was calling his walk "The Walk Against Fear."

James Meredith had been the first black student to enter "Ole Miss," the University of Mississippi, but it had taken an entire Army unit to get him into the university. After graduation, he left Mississippi and went north for awhile, but eventually he decided to return to his home state. Meredith was not affiliated with any of the national civil rights organizations. He was planning this walk on his own and intended to walk alone.

Meredith wanted to walk across Mississippi as a message to blacks that they had to overcome their fear. He wanted to show that they should not be fearful and should stand up for their rights. This was a brave act at the time since many blacks had been killed in Mississippi. Intimidation and violence were almost a daily occurrence in the lives of the 450,000 black citizens of Mississippi. They endured harsh racism and brutality. People were beaten and killed routinely in Mississippi. In 1963, Medgar Evers, a civil rights activist, had been killed in his own yard in front of his wife and children. In 1964, three civil rights workers–Andrew Goodman, Michael Schwerner, and James Chaney–had been killed. This is what was in the mind of Meredith when he made his decision to walk the 220 miles across the state. On June 6, 1966, the first day of his walk, James Meredith was shot.

The news spread across America, and all of the major civil rights organizations quickly responded. Within a few hours, the leaders of the major civil rights organizations–Dr. King (SCLC), Floyd McKissick (CORE), Roy Wilkins (NAACP), Whitney Young (Urban League) and James Forman (SNCC)–had consulted with each other and come to a decision. They agreed that they must take action against this violent incident and protest the climate where a black man cannot walk in his own home state. They decided to go to Mississippi to the spot where Meredith had been shot and continue what Meredith had begun. They would walk across Mississippi, sending the message to the black community, "Do not be afraid. Stand up and fight for what you believe in."

The day after Meredith was shot, I received a call from SCLC's national office telling me to go to Mississippi, with three or four other staff members, and set up a base of operation. They said that Dr. King was in Chicago and would be arriving in Mississippi within a few days. Since those of us in Greene County were closest to Mississippi, and we had several staff members there, it was logical for us to be the beginning of the wave of SCLC staff members reassigned to Mississippi. Five of us packed two cars with our personal belongings, as well as mimeograph machines and other office equipment, and headed to Mississippi.

Our first order of business was to set up an office, which we soon did in the back of a barber shop. The five of us then split up to find churches along the route of the march where food could be cooked and served to the marchers and where rallies could be held. We found locations along the march where the marchers could stop for the night to rest and where we could set up tents and restroom facilities. We arranged with a rental company to deliver the tents and portable toilets to each of the locations. SCLC staff and staff members from the other organizations soon arrived in Mississippi and began taking on other responsibilities, like planning the march itself.

Several thousand people marched across Mississippi, sleeping in fields or any location that we or the SNCC and CORE staff members could find that could handle such a large number of people. There were violent confrontations, especially during the early days of the march. We were beaten and tear-gassed, and churches were burned. Several young girls who had gathered at a church were attacked and tear-gassed in an unprovoked incident. Dr. King, Hosea Williams, and Joan Baez led a march with these girls downtown to protest this incident.

When Goodman, Schwerner, and Chaney were killed, their bodies had been found near Philadelphia, Mississippi, one of the towns that Meredith had intended to walk through on his way to Jackson. Our march led through Philadelphia as well, and it was here that one of the worst incidents occurred. We had arranged to set up camp in a field for the night where we were able to cook food and rest after the long walk that day. People had gone to a rally at a nearby church. Soon after they returned, the camp was attacked by police forces. People were tear-gassed, and many had to get medical treatment. Some people were taken to jail. We vacated the spot temporarily to allow the tear gas to dissipate, but we did not abandon the site, and we stayed that night.

Unfortunately, the conflict between SCLC and SNCC became more pronounced during the Meredith march. SNCC had a large presence in Mississippi. Mississippi was SNCC territory. They had been present in Mississippi since 1964 when they began the Summer Freedom Project and conducted voter registration. They established freedom schools across the Mississippi Delta and were doing good work in that area. They had recruited a large number of college students from around the country. Andrew Goodman, Michael Schwerner, and James Chaney were a part of that project. SNCC knew Mississippi well, and the people of Mississippi knew of SNCC's efforts. Because of SNCC's presence, other organizations that came in, such as SCLC and CORE, relied a great deal upon the SNCC staff in Mississippi. Some of these staff members included Bob Moses, Julian Bond and William Ricks. Stokely Carmichael was about to assume the chairmanship of SNCC from James Forman, as part of SNCC's tradition of routinely rotating its leaders.

Stokely was becoming more militant as time passed. I had witnessed this transition from the time we were in Selma and Greene County together. On June 17, Stokely was arrested leading a demonstration in Greenwood, Mississippi. Stokely was upset, and after his release from jail, he spoke at a rally. He talked about the many times he had been arrested. He said that he was tired of it, and he wasn't going to jail any more. During his speech he said that the Movement had been using the phrase, "Freedom Now," and implied that it hadn't gotten us very far. He said that black people had to take power for themselves. That night the phrase, "Black Power," was born.

Martin and the other leaders were blindsided by Stokely's action. They were not only blindsided, they were angry. Martin said to the media that it was unfortunate that Stokely had used the phrase. Roy Wilkins from the NAACP was even more upset and harsher in his comments about Stokely. The situation led Wilkins to pull out of the march. The others tried to work through a resolution of this conflict, but Stokely was unwilling to compromise on the "Black Power" phrase and the new emerging idea of black people having power. One of the negotiators was John Lewis, who was a former chairman of SNCC and was still on the SNCC staff. John, like Martin, was a firm believer in non-violence, and he feared that what Stokely was doing could potentially lead to violence. Stokely's successor, H. Rap Brown, would go even further than Stokely. While he was chairman of SNCC, H. Rap Brown would use the phrase, "Burn, Baby, Burn."

As the March Against Fear continued to wind its way towards Jackson, the conflict between SNCC and SCLC was out in the open and soon became apparent to everyone. As we marched along, the SNCC staff would yell, "Black Power." And the SCLC staff would yell back, "Freedom Now." All the way to Jackson, people heard these two phrases and saw the growing tension between the two organizations.

More and more, it was clear that SNCC wanted to control the march. They were encouraging people to use the phrase, "Black Power." I would even say that they were trying to embarrass Martin and force him into becoming more militant. I didn't want Stokely and the SNCC staff to embarrass Martin. I loved him too much to let that happen. I loved the Movement too much not to fight back. I wanted to do whatever I possibly could to make sure the march remained non-violent, so my SCLC colleagues and I kept reminding the marchers about the importance of that. We reminded them also that James Meredith had begun this walk as a protest against the violence in Mississippi.

The media began to highlight the conflict between the two organizations and raise questions about Martin's ability to control and dominate the Civil Rights Movement. I believe that the Movement began to change on that Mississippi road, and it was not the same from that point on. Because of Stokely and H. Rap Brown, we all came under more scrutiny by the

FBI. Stokely and H. Rap Brown could hardly make a move without being watched by the FBI. I think this is also when SNCC, as an organization, began to come apart. I know that by the time we reached Jackson, John Lewis had resigned from SNCC.

Thousands arrived at the state capitol in Jackson, on Sunday afternoon, June 26. They heard speeches from Dr. King, James Forman, Floyd McKissick, Stokely Carmichael, Dorothy Height, and James Meredith. Meredith had fortunately survived his wounds and had recovered enough to speak in Jackson that day at what was probably the largest rally to take place in Mississippi during the Movement. And all of this began when one man had the courage to stand up and exercise his right to walk across his home state.

As the March Against Fear concluded on that Sunday afternoon, I headed east out of Mississippi and back to Alabama. I thought of the hate and the violence that I had seen, and the lack of compassion and love shown by some of our white brothers. But I knew that I was loved. I knew that once again God had protected me and surrounded me with his love. I knew that He had delivered me through this journey–delivered me to fight another day.

1 John 4:18-19: "There is no fear in love, but perfect love casts out fear; for fear has to do with punishment, and whoever fears has not reached perfection in love. We love because He first loved us."

Chicago with Dr. King

I had two assignments in Chicago. The first was with Dr. King in 1966 and the second with Dr. Abernathy in 1968. Martin had gone to Chicago in January 1966 in an effort to support a number of community groups around the issue of housing, both in terms of the quality of housing and the fact that blacks were being discriminated against when buying and renting homes. Certain neighborhoods did not welcome blacks. There had been questions as to whether SCLC could become an effective national organization or would remain a regional one. This campaign was SCLC's first major effort in a northern city. SCLC had strong affiliate organizations in Los Angeles and Philadelphia, but we had not mounted a ground campaign in any areas outside the South.

There was debate within SCLC about whether we should take on the Chicago campaign. The staff was divided on this. Those of us who grew up in the South were mostly opposed to it, and those who were raised in the North tended to support it. The strongest advocates on the staff for going to Chicago were Diane and James Bevel and Bernard Lafayette. Diane and James lived in Chicago and had a clear picture of the problems and needs in that city, and how SCLC might be able to help. Andy Young initially had some questions, but was persuaded that SCLC should be doing more in the North.

Hosea Williams was opposed because he felt a campaign in Chicago would take away from the voter registration and political education effort in the South. Also, he was concerned that by relocating the best staff to Chicago–those staff familiar with demonstrations and direct action–if a need arose in the South, SCLC would be unprepared to rally. In some ways, he was right, because that is exactly what happened. When Meredith was shot, some staff members in Chicago had to be reassigned to Mississippi for the March Against Fear.

Ralph was not in favor of the Chicago campaign. When Martin decided to get an apartment in the ghetto on the south side of Chicago, Ralph refused to take an apartment alongside him. This was one of the first times that Ralph was not by Martin's side. Ralph was born and raised in the Black Belt of Alabama, and I think that he was more concerned about changing the South. Also, he did not want to be away from his church too much, and so he travelled back and forth between Chicago and Atlanta once the campaign started.

Normally, Ralph would be the person to go into a city just before Martin arrived and make sure the situation was right for him, and he would be the one to give the "all-clear." However, in Chicago, Andy did this instead of Ralph. Once Martin arrived in Chicago and chose a place to stay, then staff were brought in to do the organizing and come up with a plan for direct action.

I was not a part of the first wave of staff that went to Chicago. I continued my work in the Black Belt of Alabama until June when James Meredith was shot and I was reassigned to Mississippi. Martin left Chicago to complete Meredith's March Against Fear. After the march was completed, staff met at the Penn Center in South Carolina and discussed whether or not to continue the effort in Chicago. When the decision was made to continue the campaign, I was assigned to go to Chicago along with Stoney Cooks and a couple other staff members who had been working in the South.

Chicago is a beautiful city, especially in the summer. It has a spectacular skyline. There are lovely parks in the middle of downtown, and a river that runs through the city. This is the Chicago loved by residents and tourists alike. But the tourists and most residents did not usually see the part of the city where Martin was staying. I had never worked in the North before and was unaccustomed to the problems of an urban city like Chicago, where so many people were crowded together. I was used to bad housing in the South, but homes were more scattered there. In Chicago conditions seemed much worse to me. While poor people in the South could plant a garden for food and share with others, there was no place for families to do that in Chicago. There was little space, either in the apartments or outside. Children had nowhere to play. Crime and drugs were clearly visible.

The staff assigned to Chicago, besides Stoney Cooks and myself, included Andy Young, James Orange, James and Diane Bevel, and others. Bevel and Diane were there to organize the overall strategy that we would take in Chicago. James Orange's primary task was to work with the Black Stone Rangers and other gangs in Chicago. I was assigned to work with the youth, teaching them about non-violence and organizing them in general for any direct action we might take. I was also assigned to teach people how to organize. Another assignment was to work with Martin, for example, to drive him around or drive a back-up car in a motorcade.

This assignment gave me the opportunity to meet Mahalia Jackson, one of the greatest gospel singers in the world, Billy Eckstine, a renowned entertainer, and Dick Gregory, a popular comedian at that time. Mahalia Jackson and Billy Eckstine had long been supporters of Dr. King and SCLC, and they attended the rallies that we held at churches in Chicago. They both performed at one of the largest rallies at Soldier Field, where thousands came out. It was natural for them to invite Martin to their homes in Chicago for some down time, and I was thrilled to be able to accompany him when he visited them.

The Chicago campaign was the beginning of a challenge that Martin and SCLC would face over the next few years. Martin was not received in Chicago in the same way that he had been received in the South. There were many people challenging, questioning, and even criticizing him. He was not, nor were we, accustomed to this kind of reaction. One criticism that we heard was that Dr. King did not really stay in the apartment he had rented. It is true that Martin was not always in the apartment when he was in Chicago, but one of the reasons for this was that it was not always safe for him to be there. The life of the ghetto went on–the crime, the violence, the noise–even while we were there. Because of this, Martin was not able to reflect as he was accustomed to, and he needed some place where he could do that. But he did spend time at the apartment, and I do not believe the criticism was justified.

In addition to the rallies, we marched on city hall and other city and federal departments, such as HUD. We engaged in some civil disobedience, such as rent strikes–having people not pay their rent. We organized people to speak for themselves and form an ongoing organization. We did a great deal of educating, an effort primarily directed by Stoney Cooks. We taught people about basic finances, as well as financing and owning a home. Martin felt that we needed to focus on putting people into housing other than the high-rise housing that existed in Chicago. We taught people how to get money from government agencies, such as HUD, for a new type of housing.

We found that when we marched in some of the white suburbs, the anger and the hostility of the whites were more intense than we were accustomed to in the South. Although we had faced angry whites in the South, the larger crowds we faced in the Chicago suburbs were more like mobs. In the South, there was a sense that white people did not want anything to happen to Dr. King on their turf. They may have been angry and upset, but there was never a physical attack on him. But in Chicago, white people seemed not to care who Dr. King was, and he was attacked directly, with bottles and rocks thrown at him from buildings and trees.

On one occasion Martin was hit in the face with a rock. Andy had been walking in front of him, along with Bernard Lee, Martin's special assistant. It was customary in a march like this that some of us would be in this position and some of us would flank either side of the march so that people could not break into the march, which was where I was on this occasion. As Martin bent over, holding his face, the security detail surrounded him. Andy began to shout, "We need to get Martin out of here and back to the car." As we turned to get Martin back to the car, missiles were still raining down upon us. Those of us closest to Martin tried to protect him from being struck again.

As we retreated down the line on our way back to the car, the marchers could see that something had happened to Martin. Not wanting them to get out of control, we assured the marchers that he would be okay and reminded our staff along the route to keep people in formation. Once we reached the car, Bernard Lee got into it with Martin and a police driver. Andy, another staff member, and I ran alongside as the car began to pull away, trying to make sure that no other missiles could be thrown through the windows. Once the car was on its way to the hospital, we returned to the march. We were concerned about the safety of those we had brought into the white community, and Andy soon decided it would not be safe to continue our march through the angry mob.

This was not the first time that Martin had shed his blood for the cause and it would not be the last. But it was the first time that I had witnessed it. We learned later that members of a white supremacist group had infiltrated the crowds and were encouraging the violence. George Lincoln Rockwell, leader of the American Nazi Party, led a counter-demonstration to Dr. King's attempt to integrate Chicago's white suburbs.

Even though the city had provided security during our marches into the suburbs, the white suburbanites did not seem to care since they perceived what we were doing as a real threat to them. They believed that we were going to change their community by moving in a lot of poor blacks from the ghetto of Chicago. However, the issue for us was that blacks who could afford it–the middle to upper-middle class blacks–should be able to move into these suburbs. We continued our demonstrations in the city and surrounding suburbs.

Another problem for Martin and the staff was Chicago Mayor Richard Daley. Mayor Daley felt that Martin and SCLC were challenging him and his machine. He was willing to make some concessions regarding rents for public housing, but was not willing to invest any funds to improve the housing. When these concessions were not enough for Martin and SCLC, Mayor Daley became upset. His strong opposition to our efforts hindered our ability to reach people. Some of the political people that we needed to help us in our efforts were a part of the Daley machine and we were unable to get their support. We did, however, have the support of some of the churches and community groups.

It was during this time that Martin began to notice a young seminarian, Jesse Jackson, who was working with a church organization. When Jesse, who was bright and charismatic, began to support our efforts, Martin took notice of him and asked him to help organize the clergy in the city. It was by initially working with the local clergy that Jesse became a staff member of SCLC. Martin then asked him to organize a local Operation Breadbasket in Chicago.

Operation Breadbasket was an SCLC program that Fred Bennett, a friend and classmate of Martin's, ran out of the national office in Atlanta. But it wouldn't be too long before Jesse became the face and the voice of Operation Breadbasket. Jesse also undercut some of the local leaders of Chicago and soon became the spokesman for the Chicago movement. Because of Jesse's charisma and good looks, Martin asked him to become a part of the executive staff. Jesse knew how to excite a crowd and to attract the media, and it wasn't too long before Fred Bennett was assigned to other duties.

Our stay in Chicago was not a long one and we left in late summer, except for a couple staff members who stayed behind to work on voter registration with Jesse. Unfortunately, we did not have the success that Martin was hoping for. Nor did the campaign have the impact that was needed to thrust us into other northern cities, which Martin and Andy had hoped to do. The idea had been to show that SCLC could be effective in the North, and then we could move to Philadelphia and Los Angeles where SCLC had good affiliate organizations. But the lack of overwhelming success in Chicago made this impractical, and it began to raise questions about Dr. King and SCLC. This was just the beginning of the challenges that we would face as we moved forward. SCLC went back to the South, and I was reassigned again to Alabama.

My second stint in Chicago was in late August, 1968, following the Poor People's Campaign. Ralph wanted to go to Chicago because the Democratic National Convention was being held there, and he wanted to keep the issue of poverty before the American people and in their conscience while the national spotlight was on the Convention.

But the anti-war movement was also going on in Chicago at that time. The streets were crowded with all kinds of protesters, so we did not get the kind of attention that Ralph had hoped for. We didn't even get into the Convention itself, although I was able to talk before the Rhode Island delegation at their hotel. Since the anti-war protest was so huge, the networks had cameras set up at various locations around the city. During the two weeks we were there, we would drive a mule train down Michigan Avenue and through the city. The network directors would cut away and pick up our mule train for awhile, but that was about the only publicity we got.

So our presence was only a footnote compared to the Convention and the other demonstrations, one of which became known as the Chicago "police riot," when, over a period of five days and nights, hundreds of people were beaten, brutalized, and tear-gassed by police officers. All of this was done at the order of Mayor Daley. One of the major scenes from within the National Convention itself was when one of the speakers accused Daley of Gestapo tactics. Another scene was when NBC floor reporter, John Chancellor, was carried off the floor while he was reporting.

Before leaving Chicago and returning to Alabama, I met Frechettia Ford for lunch one last time. After the SCOPE project in Troy ended, she had returned to Chicago, working once again as a nurse in one of the hospitals. Connecting with her was the highlight of the Chicago assignment for me. She had shared some important moments in my life. She was there along with Leon when I walked out of jail after my first arrest. She was there offering sympathy and first aid after I had been beaten by my father. She was truly a freedom fighter, but she was more than that to me. She was my friend.

A Sabbatical to New York

From the moment that I met Leon at the beginning of the summer of 1965, I had been on the go without stopping. For well over a year, I was constantly in action, going from one place to another. As a result of the constant stress, I had developed ulcers, and I knew that I was in danger of burning out. I needed rest if I was going to be in the fight for the long haul, and I was determined to stay with SCLC and be a part of the struggle.

The writers of the Gospels all mention Jesus' need to remove himself occasionally from the crowds and seek some place to get some rest, to be refreshed. In Luke 4:42, "At daybreak he departed and went into a deserted place. And the crowds were looking for him; and when they reached him, they wanted to prevent him from leaving them." Matthew 13:1-2, "That same day Jesus went out of the house and sat by the sea. Such great crowds gathered around him that he got into a boat and sat there, while the whole crowd stood on the beach." Mark 4:35-39 "On that day when evening had come, he said to them, 'Let us go across to the other side.' And leaving the crowd behind, they took him with them in a boat."

I needed to sit by the sea, to go to the other side, and I knew that Leon and New Rochelle would be the other side for me. I had kept in touch with Leon, especially when I moved from one place to another so he would know where I was. When I thought of taking some time off to rest, my first thought was of him. He had experience in the Movement and had endured some of what I was going through. In a way, he had been my teacher. He had become a second father. I knew that if I went to New Rochelle and spent time with him, he would take care of me. We could sit together and talk, and share war stories of the battles we had been through. Being with him would allow the wounds to heal and the soul and spirit to be renewed. I could think of no better place to go and sit by the sea and receive what I needed to be recharged for the battles that lay ahead.

When I called Leon to tell him that I needed to get away for a while, he said, "You know that you are always welcome here. You will always have a place in my home." I called the SCLC office and asked for a short sabbatical, and it was approved. I learned that two volunteers from New England who had been working in Choctaw County, Alabama, were ready to return home and would be driving through New York, so I contacted them and asked if I could accompany them. They readily agreed, and I made my way from Greene County and met them in Selma. One of the workers was a woman from Boston; the other a man from Providence. The three of us drove straight through until we reached New York City. They dropped me off in the middle of the city around 11:00 p.m. in a place they thought would be easy for Leon to find.

I was suddenly scared to death, alone in this huge city late at night, and I was anxious for Leon to get to me as soon as possible. I had been in large cities before–Atlanta and Chicago–but then I was with other SCLC staff. Now I felt very self-conscious and vulnerable. I stood awkwardly on the sidewalk, watching people walk by, sure that they could see that I didn't belong there. I was dressed in my usual jeans, denim shirt and jacket–the "freedom suit" that we all wore in the Movement–and I was clutching the small bag that I was using as a suitcase.

After a few minutes, I found a pay phone and called Leon to let him know that I had arrived in the City, and tried my best to explain where I was. He gave me instructions on what to do until he got there so I wouldn't stand out so much, and suggested that I find a business that was open and wait inside. Then he and his wife Helene got out of bed and drove from New Rochelle into Manhattan to pick me up. In less than an hour, they arrived, and I was never happier to see anyone. Not just because I was safe again, but because it was so good to see Leon after all that had happened during the past year. We are both very emotional, and when we greeted each other, we hugged and cried, just as we had when we said goodbye the year before.

When I arrived at their home, I didn't know how long I would be there. How long I would be a part of the daily life of their family and a part of their social network. I was pleased to finally meet Helene and their three children, ages eight to thirteen: Susan was the oldest; Philip, the middle child; and Steve, the youngest.

I got along well with the two boys and spent some time with them, going to events or to the homes of their friends. Leon had asked the children to introduce me as their brother, and the boys seemed to have little or no problem with that. I think the member of the family who had the most difficulty with my presence was Susan. Susan had not been happy when her father had gone down South the year before. Then I was suddenly thrust upon the family and into her life. That was bad enough, but she was also asked to give up her room for me, which understandably created problems for her. Susan was just becoming a teenager, and it was difficult for her to introduce me to her friends as a member of the family. Although I was conscious of what Susan must be feeling, I was unable to express to her that I understood. All three children are now professionals, and we have kept in touch. Susan is a teacher like her parents. Philip is a doctor, and Steve is a lawyer.

In those early days the primary responsibility for me fell upon Helene. Leon and Helene were both teachers, but Helene's schedule didn't require her to be in the classroom every day at a certain hour so she had the flexibility to take me around. The clothes that I had may have been suitable for fighting for freedom, but they were not suitable for visiting Leon and Helene's friends or going into the city. Helene's first task was to take me shopping to find some clothes.

It was Helene who introduced me to the Big Apple. She introduced me to Broadway and to Harlem and its culture. She was the one who showed me the places to go and the places not to go. I realize that Helene may have had some issues about having to be the one to show me around and educate me to the life of the city, rather than Leon. But she was willing to do whatever she could to make things comfortable for me. Once Helene had shown me around the city and how to get there on the train from New Rochelle, on Saturday afternoons I would often go to the Apollo Theater where the major soul acts, such as James Brown, the Temptations, Stevie Wonder and many others, performed. So I was truly getting some respite.

From time to time Leon took me to the high school where he taught history. He arranged for me to speak to his classes and to other classes, as well as at assemblies. I was pleased to do this for him after all he had done for me. Leon always introduced me as his son. On one occasion this almost caused a riot when a group of students questioned how I could possibly be his son if I was black, with another group arguing that I could be. Leon was also a businessman, involved in residential and commercial real estate. He had apartments and office buildings, both in the city and in other localities, and he occasionally took me around with him to some of his business appointments. Leon introduced me to Judaism by bringing me with him to his temple. Prior to that, I had little knowledge of the Jewish religion, culture and traditions.

I learned so much during that visit to New York. I was able to experience a world much different from my own. Leon had given me a new life. He had given me new hope, and now he was letting me stay in his home to sit by the sea and rest, leading me to peace. I stayed with them for a few weeks, but then Birmingham became a hot spot once again and I left New Rochelle to rejoin the fight.

The Gutherz family has been a part of my life from that first day when I met Leon in my hometown, and he invited me to join him and his group in their effort to register blacks to vote. And I have been a part of their lives ever since Leon called his wife Helene and told her about me and what my father had done to me. Since those moments, we have been connected. We have been family. Leon said to me the morning after my father had severely beaten me that he would always be there for me, and he has kept his word. He and his family have been my extended family ever since.

Throughout my life, I have called upon the Gutherz for assistance and support, both on a personal level and while I was in the Movement, and they have always responded to my requests. They have sacrificed and come to those places that I have asked them to come. They have left the comfort of their lives in New Rochelle in order to support me. But even more than that, they have humbled themselves to connect, support, and speak for others less fortunate than they.

They have been there at all of the important moments of my life, when my own family wasn't able to be there because of their financial circumstances and because of the distance that separated us. Helene's passion is education, and so they were there on a cold and snowy Sunday in January when I graduated from Rhode Island College with my B.A. degree. It was Helene who had encouraged me to get an education, encouraging me as she encouraged her own children. When I graduated from seminary, Leon and Helene were both there to share the moment I received my M.Div. degree, even though they had divorced by that time. When I became pastor of a church, they came at different times to worship and support me. I have also been there for most of the major moments in their life as well. I've been there for the children's weddings, for special birthdays, and for the celebration of Leon's remarriage. The Gutherz are my family.

Birmingham

A few years ago I took my family to visit some of the battlefields where I "fought" during the Civil Rights Movement. We visited Birmingham, Alabama, with its history of horrific violence during the Movement. Because of the number of bombings that had taken place there, Birmingham had been nicknamed, "Bombingham." We stood in the park that borders the 16th Street Baptist Church, and I told my daughters about the four young girls, not much younger than they, who had been killed in 1963 when a bomb exploded at the church while they were sitting in a Sunday school class.

I was too young to have been in Birmingham that year so I did not witness the fire hoses turned upon black children and women as they protested in the park nor the dogs that were unleashed by police to attack the protesters. But as I stood there with my daughters, I remembered the violence that occurred when I was there in 1966. I could hear the cries of the children as they were sprayed with tear gas in that same park. I could hear the clicking of horses' hooves on the pavement as they chased us through the streets. I could see the police swinging their billy clubs and protesters doubling up to protect themselves as they were struck again and again.

SCLC had first gone to Birmingham in 1963 in support of the issue of public accommodation. Although the Civil Rights Act had not yet been passed, blacks throughout the South were attempting to gain access to public facilities, such as restaurants, restrooms, water fountains, bus station waiting rooms–all of which were still segregated. Birmingham, the second largest city in Alabama, had gained a reputation of being one of the most segregated cities in the South. It was during the protests in 1963 that Police Chief Bull Connor ordered the water from the fire hoses to be directed at the protesters and unleashed the dogs to attack them. People were brutally beaten and thrown in jail. Pictures of what was happening appeared in newspapers and on televisions around the country. The business community in Birmingham was unhappy with the kind of publicity and reputation that Bull Connor's actions were giving the city, and they applied pressure for an agreement on public accommodation to be reached.

After the campaign was finished, SCLC moved onto other projects, such as the voter registration campaign in Selma that led to the Voting Rights Act signed into law by President Lyndon Johnson. It was after SCLC had left Birmingham and the city dealt with implementing the negotiated agreement that the 16th Street Baptist Church was bombed, a shocking event for Birmingham and for the nation. It would be several decades before anyone would be brought to justice for this horrific act.

Once the public accommodation campaign in Birmingham had ended and the public facilities were integrated, at least theoretically, black people were usually able to go to restaurants, hotels, bus stations, and libraries, in the same way as whites. Rev. Fred Shuttlesworth, President of the Alabama Christian Leadership Conference, an affiliate organization of SCLC, had been monitoring the progress of the public accommodation effort and decided it was time to move it to the next level. Although blacks were now able to go to these places, they were still unable to work in many of them. Although the business community had ultimately been helpful with the integration agreement, they were moving very slowly in reaching out to the black community in terms of employment. Rev. Shuttlesworth and his supporters began a campaign to get people employed in these facilities.

They put pressure on the business community but continued to face stiff opposition, both from the businesses and the political structure. During their protests, Shuttlesworth and many of his supporters were arrested and beaten by Bull Connor and his police force. Finally, Rev. Shuttlesworth called Martin and asked him if SCLC could return to Birmingham to support him in his efforts to get the city to move forward, mostly with the hiring of black people in downtown businesses, but also to push for true integration of public facilities where that had not yet happened.

When the call went out that SCLC was going into Birmingham, I was still in New York with the Gutherz family. They called me and said that they wanted to put their best and most seasoned staff into Birmingham and asked if I was ready to return to action. I did not hesitate in my response, and I arrived in Birmingham in a few days. I was met at the airport by an SCLC staff member and taken to the Gaston Motel where Terrie Randolph, Stoney Cooks, and Kate Jackson from the national office staff had set up headquarters.

A. G. Gaston, the owner of the motel, was the richest black man in Alabama. If he was not the richest, then he was certainly close to the top. Besides the hotel, he owned several radio stations, a couple insurance companies, and a school. Many at the time considered Mr. Gaston an Uncle Tom, someone who would sell out the black community. But one of the things about the Movement was that there was a role for everybody. When we filled the jails, as had been done in 1963, Mr. Gaston was one of the few people who could get into the jails because of his relationship with the white power structure. From time to time, when we needed someone to bring messages from the outside to the inside, and vice versa, Mr. Gaston did that for us. Mr. Gaston passed away in 1996 at the age of 103. He outlasted both Martin and Ralph.

I felt honored to be in Birmingham during this second time that SCLC was in the city, trying to make things right. I was willing to do whatever I needed to do in memory of those who had died and those who had been scarred by the hoses and the dogs. I wondered if Bull Connor had learned anything from the experience three years earlier, when his brutality had swept into living rooms across America.

It was easier for SCLC in Birmingham the second time, because the young people who had been motivated three years before and had been trained in non-violence techniques, were still there. We had a seasoned, ready-made army in place, and all we had to do was call upon them, organize them for this new campaign, and put them back on the streets. And the young people did respond. The killing of the young girls was still fresh in the minds of the community, and was a driving force that got people to turn out. Some of the same tactics that had been used before, we used again. I was honored to help organize them and lead them into battle. I discovered that Bull Connor hadn't changed that much. He was still as easy to anger and to over-react as he had been in 1963.

We had young people marching all over the city. We marched from the park into downtown where most of the businesses were located, because it would be there, if our efforts were successful, that some of these young people or their parents would be working—working in some of the largest department stores and the hotels that catered to conventions. And hopefully, these would be meaningful jobs. We marched on city hall. We blocked traffic. We boycotted downtown businesses. The police tried to keep us from getting downtown, so we would leave on occasion from the 16th Street Baptist Church and go in several directions, thus stretching Bull Connor's forces. Young and old were beaten and tossed into jail. We filled the jails of Birmingham and two other nearby communities. We had so many people in jail that some had to be held at a nearby fairground. I went to jail with them on a number of occasions during this effort. We did this for several weeks. Martin and Ralph went to jail as they had done in 1963, but his time there would be no manifesto such as "A Letter from a Birmingham Jail."

In addition to the demonstrations taking place, we also started doing voter registration. Like Hosea Williams, Rev. Shuttlesworth felt that if you could change the political process, then the black community could make changes for itself. To that end, we set up another field office at the opposite end of the park from the Gaston Motel. The SCLC staff split into teams, with some of us continuing to work on direct action, and others working on voter registration. Occasionally, we took some of the adults directly to the courthouse after they had marched downtown. We went into the community and tried to identify those people who were registered and those who were not. We were determined to register people. Hosea believed that if more blacks were registered, we would change the dynamics of a community, thus encouraging some of the more moderate whites to step forward and run for public office and challenge some of the old hard-line politicians who had been in power for so long. Some of these moderates might even have the courage to stand up and run against Bull Connor himself.

I believe that both of these efforts were successful, for we registered thousands of people in Birmingham and people were able to get jobs in public facilities because of our actions. Even before we left, we could feel the wind of change. In the next election, some moderates were put into office on the strength of the black vote. And a few years later, Birmingham elected its first black mayor, Richard Arrington. It was incredible to see blacks in power.

Many people sacrificed a great deal and deserve much of the credit for this success. Rev. Shuttlesworth, who died in 2011, was one of the most courageous freedom fighters on the local level that I met in all of the time I was in the Movement. The brave young people who were hosed and beaten have been models, both for their own children and for other young people in the years since then. Some of the students who were in the streets with us, as well as some who watched from the sidelines, went on to be major influences in our country. Several went on to higher education, becoming deans and presidents of colleges. Many took other successful career paths. Although I do not know if she participated in any of the demonstrations, one of the most successful of the Birmingham children from that period is Condoleezza Rice, who went on to become an educator, the National Security Advisor to President George W. Bush, and Secretary of State. Those young people who came out and supported SCLC during its two stints in Birmingham helped us to change America and the world. They were all freedom fighters.

As I stood in the park and talked to my daughters, I hoped that what I and others had done all those years before had moved them. I hoped that they would see that sometimes you have to stand up and fight for what you believe in. Even if there is a cost for doing that, sometimes it is necessary to sacrifice in order to do what is right. I don't know what issues they will have to face in their lifetime, but I hope that they will remember the courage of the young people of Birmingham, and when the time comes, they will stand up and fight, whatever the cost might be.

Greensboro, Alabama

The black community in Greensboro, Alabama, wanted to see changes made in their town and throughout Hale County. They wanted a better life for themselves and their families. The black leaders decided that the black community should boycott the white-owned businesses. However, they realized the potential for danger. They knew that people had been killed in nearby Selma and Marion trying to bring about change, so they asked SCLC for assistance. I was assigned to go to Greensboro and work with the community as SCLC's project director in Hale County. At the age of twenty, I found myself directing my first major project.

As I left Birmingham and headed towards Greensboro, my mind took me back to the last time I had been in Greensboro. The year before Martin had done a brief, two-day tour through the Black Belt of Alabama. He wanted to meet with people in various towns, as well as speak at some of the larger black churches. Three of us were standing in the parking lot outside the airport in Montgomery, watching as Martin's plane descended. After the plane landed, Albert Turner and I entered the airport to greet Martin and his entourage, which included Tom Offenburger, an administrative assistant, and some of the children– Martin Luther King III, Dexter King, and Ralph David Abernathy III. I hadn't seen Martin in a little while, and it had been even longer since I'd seen the boys. We all piled into the three cars that would make up our little caravan. Martin got into the first car. Tom got into the front seat of the car I was driving, and the three children climbed into the back. Although we hadn't requested it, a state police detail was assigned to us in Montgomery, and we understood that they were to travel with us through the Black Belt.

We spent the day touring Greene County and were running a little late when we left for Selma where Martin was to speak that evening at Brown Chapel. Since Martin was scheduled to have dinner with some of the local leaders of Selma, we were speeding in order to get him there in time. However, just as we were about to leave Greene County, the state police detail unexpectedly left us. As we drove over the line into Hale County, we were surprised to be met by two police cars. Since we didn't know the arrangements for the detail, we thought perhaps the state police were handing us over to the Hale County sheriff's department to escort us through that county. Somehow Hale County seemed to know we were coming, but they obviously were not planning an escort service. Instead they were waiting for us with shotguns and machine guns drawn, and they surrounded the three vehicles. One of the children asked, "Why are we being stopped? Why do they have guns out?" I turned and looked at the boys in the back seat and said, "Everything will be all right. Don't worry." Tom tried to reassure them as well by saying, "There must be some mistake." The sheriff approached the first car which Martin was in and spoke to him. He came to my car next and told me that we were being taken into custody and were going to Greensboro.

It was late in the afternoon and almost everything had closed, so not many people were about. We were taken to jail and were informed that they would bring in a judge and a trial would be held. I was nervous for Martin's safety and kept looking around to see if I saw any black people that I could signal, to let them know that Martin was here. I felt that if the word got out in the black community that Dr. King was here, people would come to the courthouse and that would assure his safety. But I saw no one. There were no black people on the street, not even a black person at the jail. There was no way to alert the community.

In most situations, people from out of town would be given a summons to return to court later or to mail in a fine. However, this was not an option for us, and we were held in cells for several hours waiting for the judge. The children were brought into the courtroom to sit and wait. A judge finally came and we were tried, found guilty, fined and released. The three of us who were driving were charged with traffic violations. Some of the others were charged with other violations.

This was one of the few times that Martin had the children with him on the road. He only brought them when he felt that it was relatively safe. Since there were no demonstrations planned for this trip and he was just planning to greet people and make a couple speeches, this had seemed to be an opportunity for him to spend some time with his children and give them an opportunity to see what their father did. Unfortunately, they got a real taste of the danger that he encountered every day.

After our release, we proceeded to Selma, where a mass meeting was scheduled and Martin was to speak. Because of the time we spent in jail in Greensboro, Martin missed the dinner that had been scheduled, and we were late for the meeting. But once we arrived at the Brown Chapel AME Church and Martin was introduced, it seemed that he had gained new energy from our encounter with the Hale County authorities. He had Brown Chapel rocking, and there was an incredible energy and excitement in the church. I was standing with the children slightly behind Martin. As I listened to him and saw his ability to move people, I wondered how the children must feel and if they truly understood the impact that their father had on people.

As I drove into Greensboro to start my new assignment, I could not know that I would spend time in the same jail that I had been in with Martin. That I would sit in the same courtroom where the children had sat, and would be tried once again. But this time the community would know I was there, because I had been leading them into battle. This time they would stand up and speak for themselves.

But I also did not know that my personal life would change in Hale County during this second visit. I didn't know that I would learn what caring and love really meant and would experience it for the first time.

The black community in Hale County was tired of the mistreatment and the lack of respect that they had endured over the years. Even though the Civil Rights Act and the Voting Rights Act had been passed, blacks were still experiencing indignities, not only in Greensboro, but throughout Alabama. Blacks still couldn't eat in restaurants or stay at motels when traveling. Even though they were spending their money shopping for food, clothes and all of the other necessities of life, blacks were still treated badly in the stores. They could not even try on clothes before buying them.

Women were still called "auntie" or "girl" and men were referred to as "boy." The black community felt they deserved more respect.

The lack of job opportunities was another major issue for black people in Greensboro. They felt blacks should be able to work in places where they were spending their money, but none of the stores had blacks working in any kind of semi-professional position. They may have been hired as janitors or as kitchen workers, but not as waiters or waitresses in restaurants, or as clerks in department stores. That was true in all businesses and industries in Greensboro.

Most of the black leaders in Hale County were professional people. Usually, it was regular community people and the poor who stood up and fought for change, but in Greensboro the semi-professionals were on the frontline. One of the leaders was Lewis Black, head of the credit union used by blacks, who also worked for the Alabama Human Rights Commission. Another was Eugene Lyles, a barber with one of the few black businesses in the downtown area; his family also ran a grocery store downstairs from the barbershop. Theresa Burroughs, a hairdresser, was also one of the leaders. Theresa, a widow with three small children, was a very attractive, intelligent woman with many skills and leadership qualities. As a hairdresser, she had the opportunity to hear what was happening in the community—both the black and white communities—so she was in a position to provide helpful information about the needs in the community. These three were the primary leaders, although others, including some clergy, were involved as well.

When I arrived, I talked to the leaders, assessed the situation, and determined where to go from there. It was important for me to determine the real leader—that is, the one that people really listened to. Although people can be identified as a leader or can identify themselves as a leader, they may not really have the influence. It became clear to me fairly soon that the real leader was Theresa Burroughs. Mr. Black often ran the meetings, but it was Theresa who had the vision. When she spoke, people listened. However, the situation in Greensboro was the same as in most communities. The women deferred to the men and stayed in the background. In some ways, this was true for Theresa, although she was strong and spoke up when she felt the men weren't providing a clear direction and vision.

We soon instituted the boycott. We found pastors who supported our efforts and allowed us to hold mass meetings at their churches. Our "headquarters" church was St. Marks in Greensboro, a large church which held several hundred people. At these mass meetings we encouraged people to withhold their money from white-owned businesses. At one of the first mass meetings at St. Marks, I told the audience, "We are not going to spend our money where our women are being disrespected and abused." I added, "Men, we must respect our women, and we must stand up for them. We have to fight for fairness and dignity." As I reflect on that speech, I wonder what the men thought of a twenty-year old, telling them how to treat women! We spoke at churches and to community groups in Greensboro and throughout Hale County, urging people not to shop in Greensboro, except to pay their utility bills. We encouraged them to shop out of town, which meant going to Demopolis, Marion, or Eutaw, all of which were about twenty miles from Greensboro. As part of our education effort, we also distributed flyers and a newsletter.

We instituted some direct action, by setting up picket lines and demonstrations throughout the downtown area. We told people that we were not going to spend our money in Greensboro until blacks could work downtown. We picketed stores, such as dress shops, and we even picketed the town hall and county courthouse. But we picketed daily at Adams Market, one of the largest grocery stores, since it had a history of mistreating black customers. As the boycott went on, I encouraged Mr. Lyles to expand the goods in his small family grocery store so that people could shop there as an alternative to shopping out of town. He was willing to do this, but was unable to get all of the goods he needed because Wesley "Doc" Adams, the owner of Adams Market, was pressuring the suppliers not to sell to him. We told Mr. Lyles that we would organize caravans to go to Tuscaloosa to pick up the supplies he needed, and we made this eighty-mile roundtrip several times.

It was clear to me that women had the buying power in the county. They were the ones who bought food and clothes for the family. I felt that their voices especially needed to be heard because of the lack of respect they had been shown by merchants. Theresa and three other women–Dorothy, Delois, and Martha Ann–were a voice for the black women in Greensboro. They were willing to fight for what they believed was right and for the dignity of black people in Hale County, and they supported me in my efforts. We pounded the pavement every day for weeks and weeks. Sometimes we would have simultaneous picket lines on opposite ends of town. Besides Theresa, I knew that these three women had my back and that I could count on them day or night.

One of the things about picketing is that as long as you don't interfere with people entering and exiting buildings, normally you can do it without being arrested. But occasionally you will be arrested even when you abide by the rules, or the police will try to limit the number of people allowed to picket at a given site. We were sometimes arrested, even though we were clearly peaceful and courteous to all who wished to get by, either on the sidewalks or entering an establishment. I was arrested a couple times, once while picketing Adams Market.

When we picketed, we had signs or placards stating our message since we weren't engaging with people individually. These signs stated our demands and why we were picketing. One of our signs made reference to the Ku Klux Klan, and on the occasion when I was arrested at Adams Market, I was carrying that sign. It read, "Why support the KKK?" I had decided that I should be the one to carry the sign, because it was such a provocative message. If an onlooker became upset about it and tried to attack whoever was holding the sign, I wanted them to come after me and not one of the women picketing. I had been trained how to protect myself when attacked, but the women had not.

I was very familiar with the emblem of the Ku Klux Klan, and I had seen that there was a Klan emblem on Mr. Adams' car. That was the reason for the message on the sign. When I was arrested, I was charged with criminal libel since Mr. Adams denied that he was a Klansman. He said that he was a member of the White Citizens Council and further stated that the emblem on his car did not say KKK, but KKN, which was the beginning of his radio operator's license number. The White Citizens Council was a "brother" organization to the Ku Klux Klan. Members of the White Citizens Council didn't wear hoods, they were not as brutal as the Ku Klux Klan, and they usually didn't burn churches. But most members supported the Klan and turned their eyes away from what the Klan did.

This case dragged on for quite a while. Later when I was arrested in other communities, the case would keep coming up because it had never been settled since I was being sued personally. Eventually, I pled guilty to a lesser charge of trespass because there were very few blacks in the jury pool and it was clear that even though we could produce the necessary evidence, a white jury would not find in my favor.

We kept up the pressure on the business community and on government officials to insure that blacks would be hired in various positions throughout the business community. We were determined to make sure that this became a reality, because in the past SCLC often reached an agreement of understanding in a community, only to have officials renege on the agreement. In Greensboro we wanted to see people at work in these jobs before we called off the boycott and allowed things to return to normal.

Although we wanted blacks hired throughout Greensboro, one of the first places we wanted to see people working was at Adams Market. People had strong feelings about the market, because of the mistreatment that black people experienced while shopping there. It would be symbolic of our success if this was one of the first places that a black face could be seen working. Then the employment of blacks could spread outward from there.

While we were picketing, black people continually applied for positions at Adams Market and all of the other stores downtown. We trained people how to dress appropriately for an interview and how to conduct themselves during the interview. Finally, after about three months of picketing, we were successful in getting black people hired in Greensboro. The very first hires were mostly women, who were hired as sales clerks in some of the shops. Although it took Mr. Adams a little longer, finally he hired a black man as a meat cutter, and soon both men and women were hired as cashiers at the market.

After we resolved the issue of employment, I stayed in Greensboro to work on other issues of concern in the community and throughout Hale County. Although the Civil Rights Act had been passed, there was still little opportunity for blacks to go out and socialize, since few restaurants were accessible to them. Hardly any recreational outlets existed for blacks, particularly those who lived in rural areas.

There was no public playground or recreation facility open to black or minority children. However, there was a swimming pool on the edge of town that appeared to me to be a public facility. I had scouted out this facility, and I never saw that any white children wanting to go in were denied access because they were not members. So one afternoon I decided that we should test this facility. I gathered a small group of black youths, and we went to the swimming pool to see if we would be admitted or would be denied the right to swim. The group of young people with me included two of Theresa's children and her niece. I had decided that we would not put ourselves in the position of being arrested, since I hadn't cleared that with the parents of the young people. We were denied access and were told that it was a private facility. I didn't believe the woman who spoke to us, and I told her that we would return, that it would not be the last time they would see us. This is just one example of what life was like for blacks in Hale County.

There was a wide chasm between whites and blacks in Hale County in the area of education, although this was an issue statewide. In fact, I took on Lurleen Wallace, the Governor of Alabama at that time. She had stepped in to fill the office when her husband George could not run for governor again without taking a break, although in subsequent years he did become governor once again. At the time Lurleen was threatening to defy a federal court order to desegregate the school districts in Alabama. I was quoted in the local newspaper as saying, "If Lurleen stands in the schoolhouse door, I'm going to make it my personal business to stand in the door with her, to make sure black children get into the schools. If she calls out the National Guard, I'm going to call the SCLC staff back into Alabama." Eventually, she backed down when she realized that the government would send in the military to enforce the federal court order. From there, we began to work on education issues, trying to improve the quality of education for all the children of Hale County, but particularly for black students. We made some inroads on education throughout the county. We were able to force the county to provide better textbooks for all students. We were able to get money from the State of Alabama which was used to provide scholarships to high school graduates to attend technical school.

I was also involved with organizing black farmers in the area. One of their problems was money, or the lack of it. I helped them form a co-operative so that they could share their financial resources to purchase farm machinery that could be used by all of them. Another important issue was getting them more assistance from the U. S. Department of Agriculture. The Department of Agriculture had extension services throughout the country that, in addition to financial assistance, provided technical assistance, such as how to manage a farm, how to irrigate fields, and so forth. However, these extension services were staffed by local people, and black farmers in the South were not getting the help they needed. We began going as a group to complain at the extension service and then went over their heads to the regional office for help. Our efforts were moderately successful. By the time I left, they were beginning to get some technical assistance and some help in preparing applications for financial assistance. I don't know how successful they were in getting loans, however, because of the discriminatory environment at the U. S. Department of Agriculture for many years.

All in all, I would say that we were successful in Hale County and that the quality of life for the black people of Hale County began to improve. During this time, I was promoted to Assistant Field Secretary for Alabama, and Greensboro became a base of operation for me as I traveled throughout the state.

Whenever I was near Troy, I would try to stop and visit my mother. My father and I had been estranged ever since he had severely beaten me when I joined SCLC in 1965. Although I kept in touch with him by phone, our relationship wasn't what it had been. But on this visit, I went to his home hoping that somehow we could reconcile. I wasn't sure how we would react to one another, but as I walked up to the door and entered his house, I was stunned at what I saw. There on his living room wall were two pictures—one of Dr. King and beside it, one of me. This was a 180-degree turn for my father. He apologized to me and said that he had been wrong. He had recently seen me on television, confronting a Klansman. He saw that I had courage and realized I was fighting for what I believed in. That was a moment of change for him. It was a redeeming moment.

Having Greensboro as my base of operations was important to me because, during the boycott, I had developed a personal relationship with Theresa Burroughs. Although I had my own apartment in Greensboro, I now had someone to spend time with when I came back from finishing a project elsewhere in Alabama. It was quite clear to everyone that we were more than casual friends and that the relationship had changed from a relationship between an organizer and supporter to a relationship between a man and woman.

Theresa was very stylish and dressed like a woman from a big city, like Atlanta or Birmingham, as opposed to a rural community in the Black Belt of Alabama. She believed in purchasing good, quality clothes, knowing that they may cost a little more, but would last longer. Fashion was not something that I had ever been concerned about since I had grown up poor and we could not afford nice clothes. It was Theresa who taught me about fashion and how to look for quality. In the Movement, we had to travel light and carried only the necessities since we could be given new assignments at a moment's notice. Along with everybody else in the Movement, I wore my "freedom suit." But once I started going out with Theresa, it wasn't always appropriate to wear jeans and work boots. I needed other kinds of clothes as well. It was Theresa who introduced me to Florsheim shoes, which she bought for me.

We were together frequently in town, and we were together out of town as well. As an Air Force widow, she went to the Maxwell Air Force base to shop, and I usually went with her. Theresa lived with the three children in a modest three-bedroom home in the western section of town. The house had a fairly large yard with a huge field out back. Her beauty shop was next to the house. If she was out, I would stay with the children and people would see the children and me together. I think we were both conscious of the children and the impact of our relationship on them. When I was in town, the five of us would often eat dinner together. If her hair appointments ran late, I would eat with the children before she came home.

Theresa was not on the picket line the day I was arrested at Adams Market. When word of my arrest reached her, she immediately came to the courthouse. She stood outside and looked up at me in my jail cell on the second floor. While I looked down upon her, we talked about what to do next. She asked me how I was doing and said that she would contact the NAACP lawyers to let them know that I was in jail and what the charges were. I asked her to also contact Albert Turner, SCLC's field secretary for Alabama. I said to her, "Keep them walking, and make a couple phone calls to get more people on the street." Less than an hour later I could hear voices in front of the courthouse, singing. As I listened, I knew that we could sustain this as long as we needed to.

I was comfortable being in jail, knowing that I would be safe because many people had seen me arrested and knew that I was there. It was not like the first time I had been in this jail with Dr. King when no one in the community knew we were there. This was a very emotional moment for me. It was the first time since I had been in the Movement that I had someone waiting for me, who really cared about me and who I cared about. It was the first time that I had somewhere to go once I was released. Normally, when I got out of jail, I would spend time with colleagues or would be alone in my room. Now it was different.

This was the first and only time I became involved with anyone in the many communities where I worked, either before or since. There was a difference in age that occasionally we had to deal with, but other than that, I felt committed. I had fallen in love for the first time in my life. I had someone who I cared about and who I believed cared about and loved me. But there was a major obstacle to our making a total commitment to our relationship. Theresa was a military widow and the mother of three. If she had married me, she stood to lose everything.

She would have lost the benefits that she was receiving to support and care for her children. At the time I didn't understand that. Even though I was going to the base with her, shopping for groceries and other things, I didn't understand what was at stake. I didn't understand that she couldn't just pack up and move away with me. And that is what I was asking her to do—to sacrifice her children's education and their livelihood and to remove them from their community. I was also asking her to give up being a leader and taking care of people in her hometown. It was clear that the people of Greensboro and Hale County needed her, needed both her caring and her leadership. I was young and naïve then, but as I have reflected on it over the years, if Theresa had done what I wanted her to do, then she wouldn't have been the woman that I loved.

But Theresa was wise enough and loved me enough to know that I couldn't stay with her either—that my future was at stake. My relationship with SCLC would be damaged if I remained in Greensboro. I know now that I wouldn't have grown, if I had stayed. I probably would never have graduated from college or gone to seminary. I would never have had the opportunity to travel the world and visit Paris, Stockholm, or Greece. Theresa encouraged me to move on, to leave her and search for my dream. Nevertheless, I could not give up my hope that somehow we might be together again.

Later during the Poor People's Campaign, when SCLC staff members were being assigned throughout the country, I asked to work in Providence, Rhode Island. A personal reason for requesting this assignment was because Theresa's sister Alberta lived there, and I hoped that Theresa might be willing to come to Providence, since she had family there. When I told Theresa that I was moving to Providence, she said that she might come after the school year had ended, So when I arrived in Providence, I had renewed hope that Theresa and I could be together forever. For the first time, someone else was part of my plans for the future, and I rented a three-bedroom apartment in Providence for us with room for the children. But then it became clear that she was not going to come.

I was broken-hearted. Alberta knew how I felt about Theresa, and she knew that Theresa's feelings for me were strong as well. When I talked to Alberta about our relationship, she would say, "You just need to go and physically force her to come, otherwise she will always find some reason not to leave since she has been in Alabama her whole life." She would also say, "Theresa will let love pass her by if you don't shake her up." But I knew this kind of action wouldn't help. I knew Theresa was committed to the community and that was a large part of who she was—being able to serve others. When I finally accepted that Theresa was not going to come, I was hurt and empty, and I vowed "never again." But for years after the relationship ended, I still had a kind of connection with Theresa and could sense when something was wrong—when she was sick or when she faced difficulties—and I would check with Alberta to make sure that Theresa was all right.

The last time I visited Greensboro was about ten years after I had left. I was showing my brother Henry Lee some of the places where I had worked when I was with SCLC. I showed him where Viola Liuzzo had been shot, and we went to a museum in Selma where my name appeared on the wall. And the next day we went to Greensboro. I showed him around town, the jail, and then we visited Theresa's home. It was good to see her again and catch up on what was happening with her and the children. She told me about the housing corporation that she had formed and the plans to build decent homes for several families on the land behind her house and shop. We visited some of her neighbors that I had known. At the end of our visit, my brother and I drove away. But after a few minutes I stopped the car along the road, got out and looked back. And I finally said goodbye to Theresa.

MY MOTHER,
MATTIE LUE REYNOLDS

MY FATHER, HENRY
REYNOLDS, AND HIS
WIFE, PATSY

THE AUTHOR AT RESURRECTION CITY,
WASHINGTON, DC, 1968

LEON AND HELENE GUTHERZ MARCHING DURING THE POOR PEOPLE'S CAMPAIGN IN WASHINGTON, DC, 1968

HELENE GUTHERZ ESTABLISHING A "FREEDOM SCHOOL" AT RESURRECTION CITY, WASHINGTON, DC, 1968

TENTS AT RESURRECTION CITY IN A SEA OF MUD, 1968

RALPH ABERNATHY, WITH MARY MOULTRIE, ON HIS RELEASE FROM JAIL AFTER A SETTLEMENT HAD BEEN REACHED IN THE HOSPITAL WORKERS STRIKE, CHARLESTON, SOUTH CAROLINA, 1969 (COURTESY OF THE WARING HISTORICAL LIBRARY, MUSC, CHARLESTON, S.C.)

A CLASS AT THE FREEDOM SCHOOL FOR NATIVE AMERICANS IN RIDGEVILLE, SOUTH CAROLINA, 1969

THE AUTHOR, PROVIDENCE,
RHODE ISLAND, 1970

IN A PROVIDENCE NEWSROOM,
GETTING PUBLICITY FOR SCLC, 1970

MY FATHER AND I,
A COUPLE YEARS BEFORE
HIS DEATH IN 1993

LEON GUTHERZ (MY SECOND
FATHER) AND I AT BETHANY
BAPTIST CHURCH, PAWTUCKET,
RHODE ISLAND, SOON AFTER I
BECAME INTERIM PASTOR, 1997

TWO FREEDOM FIGHTERS FROM TROY, ALABAMA — JOHN LEWIS AND JOHN REYNOLDS — TAKEN AT BROWN UNIVERSITY, 1999

THE AUTHOR, STILL FIGHTING THE "GOOD FIGHT," PROVIDENCE, 1993 (COURTESY OF THE PROVIDENCE AMERICAN)

GLORIA AND I ON OUR WEDDING DAY, BROWN
UNIVERSITY, PROVIDENCE, RHODE ISLAND, 1985

GLORIA AND I RELAXING AND
ENJOYING LIFE TOGETHER, AT A
SOCIAL GATHERING IN FOSTER,
RHODE ISLAND, 1995

Dr. King's Vision of a Poor People's Campaign

Dr. King had come up with the idea of organizing poor people–bringing together all of the poor, regardless of race or ethnicity–Hispanic, Native American, white, black. In the past when SCLC talked about poverty and poor people, the discussion mostly centered on black people. But it was clear that there were more poor white people than poor black people in the United States. And that was the case, not just in the South, but all over the country.

Dr. King felt that bringing people together and uplifting the issue of poverty to America would help to eliminate some of the conflicts that existed between the different groups. Race and ethnicity separated people. Blacks stayed in their corner and whites stayed in theirs, even though both groups were suffering. If the different groups could be brought together, the power structure couldn't continue to divide people into separate camps.

Dr. King wanted to overcome the kinds of issues that separated people. He wanted to organize a new force in this country that had not existed before. He wanted America to face the reality of poverty and the conditions that poverty brought about. He wanted to raise the issues between the haves and the have nots. He was calling for America to think seriously about redistributing the wealth in this country. He was concerned that so few controlled the resources, while the majority of people were barely surviving.

On February 21, 1968, at a speech in Albany, Georgia, Dr. King talked about going to Washington. He said, "We are going to start a movement. And we're not going to Washington just for one day. No, no, we are going in a wait-in and stay-in movement. Come young and old, come sick and well, come to Washington. We are going to build a shantytown in Washington. And we're going to let the whole world know what it means to be poverty-stricken. We're going to let the whole world know how America is treating its poor citizens."

This was something Martin had been concerned about for awhile. It wasn't a sudden idea for him. He had seen poverty in rural areas throughout the South during SCLC's many projects, and even before that, when he visited Coretta and her family in Alabama. But I suspect that it was his stay on the south side of Chicago that may have affected him more. I know that the large numbers of people living in poverty in the housing projects of that urban ghetto greatly affected me.

Martin understood that some of the other issues we had been working on were not going to come into full fruition until the lives of people were improved, until America had done something about the poor in this nation. Robert Kennedy and George McGovern had also gone to Mississippi and had seen the conditions there. Theirs were the only political voices speaking out on behalf of the poor. Martin felt that he could shine a bright light on this dark national secret and help people understand that poverty was not the fault of individual people, but was much more of a systematic condition.

Martin talked to the board of directors about his plan. It would mean a shift in direction for SCLC. SCLC had never conducted a national campaign before. Most of its campaigns had been state by state, or regional, like the SCOPE project of 1965 that I became involved with. There was not total agreement that SCLC should take this on, either within the board or among the members of the executive staff, who would be the ones to carry out the plan.

Martin also talked to the staff. I was more supportive than some of the others about the idea of going to Washington and for SCLC to try something different in order to improve the lives of poor people. I knew what it was like to be hungry and not have food in the house. I knew what it was like to be ashamed of the clothes you wore or the fact that your shoes had holes in the soles, because this was my life as a young boy. I did not understand all of the economic ramifications, but I knew that this would be something we all had to learn a great deal more about if we were to organize people and motivate them to go to Washington. It would be different from the other times that SCLC had gone to Washington. This time we would be asking people to make sacrifices in order to come with us and live there for an extended period of time.

At one of the planning meetings I attended, I will never forget how divided the group was and the kinds of questions that were being raised. But I will also not forget Martin's determination to move this forward and his struggle with trying to put his plan together. We were all sitting around in a conference room just outside of Martin's office on the first floor of SCLC headquarters. Martin was sitting at the head of the table, with Ralph on his right. Bernard Lafayette, who had come on board to be SCLC's program director, was on Martin's left. Andy was next to Ralph, and Hosea was next to Bernard. Jesse Jackson and Dorothy Cotton were at the other end of the table. James Orange and I, representing the field staff, sat on the left-hand side of the room, back from the table.

The discussion went back and forth about why we should go and why we shouldn't. We realized that the project would need enormous resources, both material and financial, and some doubted that we had enough staff to make it work. Also, some staff members did not want to leave their current projects to take this on. Some questioned whether we could organize and pull all of these diverse groups together and train them in non-violence. There was concern about what might happen in Washington if we weren't able to do a good job in preparing people.

The struggle for Martin was not so much tactics or whether we could organize people. His struggle had to do with President Lyndon Baines Johnson. President Johnson had been a major supporter of the Civil Rights Act, and particularly the Voting Rights Act, when he had gone on national television, saying, "We shall overcome." By going to Washington, we would be confronting the government, and therefore President Johnson. Martin had confronted President Johnson before with his opposition to the Vietnam War, and he was feeling that here again he would be confronting the president and causing him embarrassment. Although Martin was concerned about this, his desire to bring about change was stronger than that concern. He felt that we had to go to Washington even though it might cause some problems for the president.

As the meeting went on and Martin allowed people to express their opinions, at times it became somewhat heated. I looked across the room and saw that Ralph was dozing off. I wondered how he could doze off during such a heated conversation, but I knew he was one of those people who could doze off anywhere, anytime. But as the meeting and discussion continued, Ralph woke up and suddenly pushed his chair back from the table, saying, "We're going. We're going. That's it. Martin wants to go, and we're going." And then he walked out of the room and went back to his office. Soon after, Martin got up and went to his office, leaving the rest of the staff in the conference room to try and hash out what we might be able to do.

This is just one example of how we worked, and it is also an example of how Ralph supported Martin. And when Ralph spoke, we all took it seriously. We all knew that whatever our feelings might be, we had to put them aside because the decision had been made. Ralph was not a tactician, but he had the moral authority and an ability to persuade the staff.

Martin and Ralph had been to Marks, Mississippi, considered by many to be one of the poorest places in the country. They were moved by what they saw and experienced. Therefore, once the decision was made to move forward with the Poor People's Campaign, they decided that the campaign would start off from Marks, Mississippi.

I began to think about where I wanted to work, whether I wanted to work in Alabama or Georgia or someplace else. Since this was going to be a national campaign, I knew that staff would be spread out all over the country, from east to west, south to north. I felt that it might be good for me to work outside of the South. I wanted to experience the North again, but I didn't want to be in a huge city like Chicago or New York. I was looking for something smaller, so I asked Martin if I could go to Providence. I had gone to Providence with him once, and I felt that Providence was small enough that I would be comfortable working there. There was also, of course, the consideration that Theresa's sister lived in Providence.

Martin was initially resistant to my suggestion, primarily because he wasn't sure whether there were enough black people and poor people to invest the time and resources in Providence. But I persisted, and this time Bernard Lafayette, who had come from the Boston area, suggested to Martin that I could work both Boston and Providence since the cities were fairly close to one another. Martin ultimately agreed that I could set up base in Providence, but that I would have to work in Boston as well. He said that I could ask for more staff help if I needed it. Rev. Virgil Woods, one of SCLC's board members, lived in Boston, and it was arranged that he would be my contact there.

I arrived in Providence in January 1968. As I drove north on Interstate 95, through what is known as the Thurbers Avenue curve, I was able to see the skyline of Providence and knew that I was entering the home of Roger Williams. In 1636, Roger Williams had escaped from the Massachusetts Bay Colony because of religious persecution, and he founded Providence upon the principle of religious freedom and the separation of church and state. Two years later he established the first Baptist church in America. As I got closer to the city, I could see the State House, which sits on a hill overlooking the city. At the top of the State House dome is a gold-covered, bronze statue known as "The Independent Man." Rhode Island was the first colony to declare its independence from England. It has always represented freedom and tolerance. Its birth centered around religious freedom, which is why the first Jewish synagogue in America was built in Rhode Island. As I thought about pulling people together and organizing the poor, I felt that I was in the right place—a place where people were respected and were given a certain amount of dignity. It was with that in mind that I began to introduce myself to Providence and its people.

One of the first things I did was to contact Charlie Baldwin, the chaplain at Brown University, whom I had met with Martin. Charlie helped me recruit several Brown students to assist in the project. I also made contact with a social worker in Providence who had come down South in 1965 during the SCOPE project. I soon discovered that two other people that I had met down South also lived in Providence and were in a position to be very helpful.

I had met Michael vanLeestan in Selma during the summer he had worked in Coffee County, Alabama. At the time he was a student and star basketball player at Rhode Island College, the college that I would graduate from several years later. Michael was now the Executive Director of the Opportunities Industrialization Center, and he was very helpful to me in setting up in Providence and getting operations going for the

Poor People's Campaign. The other person in Providence that I had met in Alabama was Clifford Monteiro. Cliff had been a Providence police officer, but was now working with the Rhode Island Council of Churches as a community specialist. Once I had connected with Michael and Cliff, I felt better knowing that there were two local people who knew how SCLC operated. They had knowledge and skills that I could call upon to assist in identifying other leaders in the community and they could also help me find resources.

I established an office in the Pond Street Baptist Church in South Providence, an area where the majority of blacks in Providence lived, and I got to work organizing people in Providence and Boston. For the next couple of months, with the help of my volunteer assistants, I recruited people to go to Washington and made arrangements with individuals and organizations to supply us with material, food, and first aid supplies while we were in Washington. Everything was on schedule for us to travel to Washington the second week of April.

The Death of Dr. King

It had been a mild winter in Rhode Island by New England standards. Very little snow had fallen that year, and by late March, spring was already in the air. It had been a busy time for me the past few weeks. I had been running back and forth between Providence and Boston, making sure that everything was in place for the Poor People's Campaign. Martin was busy with the campaign as well. He was traveling from coast to coast, recruiting people and raising money. He had gone to Appalachia to recruit poor whites, to Oklahoma to recruit Native Americans, and to New Mexico to recruit Hispanics. It was a busy and exciting time for all of us in SCLC. This new campaign was perhaps one of the most challenging that we had undertaken. We were talking about poverty and wealth and how that wealth should be distributed.

In the meantime, the sanitation workers in Memphis, Tennessee, most of whom were black and poor, had gone on strike on February 12, 1968. They were paid very low wages and their working conditions were difficult. Rev. James Lawson, pastor of the Centenary Methodist Church in Memphis, asked Martin to come to Memphis in support of the workers. Rev. Lawson, described by Martin as "the leading theorist and strategist of non-violence in the world," had played an active role in the early sit-in movement and had worked with SCLC in Birmingham. Although the Poor People's Campaign was scheduled to kick-off during the latter part of March, Martin went to Memphis to speak at a rally on March 18. The workers and the crowd were

121

enthusiastic. Rev. Lawson and other clergy were putting plans together for a march through the city to draw attention to the plight of the workers and put pressure on the city as a way of reaching a settlement. They asked Martin to come back to Memphis for the march.

Hosea and Andy objected to his going, feeling that Martin didn't have the time to go to Memphis just as we were about to launch the Poor People's Campaign. But Martin felt that it would not be right to go to Washington and talk about the poor, but not go to Memphis to support the sanitation workers who were poor and were trying to improve their situation. So on March 22, Martin, Ralph, and Bernard Lee went to Memphis to participate in the march and give support to the workers. Since SCLC staff was scattered all over the country working on the campaign, none of us went to Memphis with them to provide support. They were on their own, except for the local black community in Memphis.

Fairly soon after the march began, there were signs of trouble. As Martin and Ralph led the march, violence erupted in the rear. Bricks were being tossed through the windows of businesses along the route. A black gang known as the Invaders, upset at being excluded, had infiltrated the march in order to cause trouble. The media was critical in their reporting of the incident, and they began to raise questions. They asked how Dr. King could safely take thousands of people to the nation's capital when he couldn't even control a march in Memphis. Martin felt that he and his non-violence philosophy were being tested. He was determined to return to Memphis to prove that non-violence was still effective and that he was as committed to it as he had been from the very beginning in Montgomery.

This time some staff were pulled out of Georgia, Alabama and Mississippi, and they went to Memphis to prepare for a second march. They were confronted with a number of problems, including a court order banning marches. James Orange and James Bevel worked on getting the Invaders under control, while Hosea Williams and Andy Young worked with the larger community and their leaders.

April 3 was a stormy night, and a mass meeting was scheduled at the Mason Temple. Martin had sent Ralph to the church to speak, but once Ralph got there, he called Martin and said, "Martin, you have to come. The people want you." Martin came over and that night gave his final speech, "I've Been to the Mountain Top," which ends with these prophetic words:

"Like anybody, I would like to live a long life. Longevity has its place. But I'm not concerned about that now. I just want to do God's will.

And He's allowed me to go up to the mountain. And I've looked over. And I've seen the Promised Land.

I may not get there with you. But I want you to know tonight, that we, as a people, will get to the promised land! And so I'm happy tonight. I'm not worried about anything. I'm not fearing any man! Mine eyes have seen the glory of the coming of the Lord!!"

On the morning of April 4, I woke and looked out the window of my apartment in Providence. It was a beautiful New England day. I had a busy schedule planned for the day. I had a staff meeting that morning, and later in the morning I had a meeting at the National Guard headquarters to finalize details for the use of the Cranston Street Armory for the New England kick-off of the Poor People's Campaign. A mass meeting was scheduled for that night. In some ways I thought it would be just a routine day. But I should have realized, as long as I had been in the Movement, that there is no such thing as a routine day.

After my two meetings in the morning, I went back to my apartment and decided I would work from there that afternoon since I was expecting a shipment of material from SCLC's national office, which I planned to distribute at the meeting that night. By mid-afternoon I began to get upset because the material had not arrived, and I started pacing the floor. Finally, after calling UPS and checking on the shipment, I put in a call to SCLC and spoke with Martin's secretary, Dora McDonald, expressing concern that I hadn't gotten the supplies. She assured me that the material was on its way and that I should have it in time for the meeting.

But something else was worrying me. I had wanted Martin to come to Rhode Island to promote the campaign, and I had finally gotten a commitment from him that he would come. But since we hadn't yet settled on a date, I was worried that he might not show up. I was afraid that Andy might convince him that his time would be better spent elsewhere. So I asked Dora if Martin still had me on his schedule. She assured me that Rhode Island and Massachusetts were on his schedule.

I hadn't seen Martin since mid-January when we were putting final plans together for the campaign. In my frustration that afternoon, I didn't think about what he was doing that day in Memphis. I never imagined that this would be a day I would remember for the rest of my life. We all knew that Martin's life was threatened almost daily. But none of us wanted to think about it all the time. We knew what was possible. But at the same time, it seemed impossible. This man, who had become so important to me personally, was so vibrant and full of life. He was still so young–only thirty-three years old.

It had gotten late in the afternoon. I was beginning to think about where I would go to eat before the mass meeting. Unknown to me, Martin and Ralph had been thinking the same thing at the Lorraine Motel. But before I came to a decision, the phone rang. I was hoping that it was UPS saying that my material was on the way. But when I answered the phone, I recognized the voice on the other end. It was Valerie Raymond, a Brown University student from Long Island, who had been working with me on community outreach and fundraising. Valerie asked me if I was watching television. I told her, "No, I don't have the television on." I had no idea what she was about to tell me. She said, "Then you haven't heard!" "Heard what?" I asked. I was getting impatient; I didn't have time for games. What she said next hit me to the core of my soul. She said, "Dr. King has been shot in Memphis!" That was all she knew. I told her that I would call SCLC's national office and get more information, and asked her to call me back.

After I hung up, I turned on the television and called SCLC. The operator patched me through to Claudette Mathews, the office manager, who confirmed that Martin had been shot, but she knew very little of what had happened. She and the others were waiting for a call from Andy or Hosea. I asked her to get back to me when she had more information. I took a moment to catch my breath, because my chest was pounding. As I turned around to face my little TV, a bulletin came on the screen and Chet Huntley reported that Dr. King was dead.

I fell on my knees in front of the television. Tears began to run down my face, and I cried out in pain and anger that someone had taken Martin from us, but I was also filled with grief at my personal loss. I was on my knees for a while, and then I could hear the phone ringing in the background. I wondered at first if it was Claudette, but then I realized that it was too soon for her to call me back. She had to be experiencing what

I was experiencing at the moment. It would be difficult for her. She saw Martin almost every day that he was in the office. When he had left for Memphis, she would have been the one to give him his ticket. I hesitated before picking up the phone. It was Valerie getting back to me. She told me that she and some of the others who had been working with me were on their way. The phone kept ringing. I answered some of the calls, but not all. I was still in too much pain. After Valerie and the others arrived, they took over answering the phone. One of the calls was from Cliff Monteiro saying that he was on his way over to be with me.

I was still in shock by what had happened, and I didn't know what to do. As I watched television, I could see that violence was taking place around the nation. I knew that I had a responsibility to Martin's vision and to non-violence. I knew that I needed to try to keep a lid on the situation in Rhode Island. The group in my apartment talked about what we should do, how we should respond. Cliff suggested that we ask people to come to the State House. They could come to the seat of power in Rhode Island in a peaceful and non-violent way, and I could grieve along with them. Before we went to the State House, I asked Valerie to call the church where we had planned to have the mass meeting that night. I didn't want people to gather at the church or in the streets around the church, because I didn't want the possibility of any violence taking place there. I wanted people either to go home or to come to the State House.

A short while after we arrived at the State House, I was looking up into the rotunda when a capitol policeman came over to inform me that a few incidents of violence had begun taking place in South Providence. I knew that I needed to go to there, and so Cliff and I, with several other men, left the State House and drove to South Providence. We tried to calm people down, encouraging them to go home or come to the State House with us. We told them that Dr. King would not be pleased if violence erupted in the community. Violence was not his way, and it was not the way to honor him. We told them that it would be the community that would suffer because the police would lock down the area. After an hour or so, walking the streets, we returned to the State House where I stayed until I left for Dr. King's funeral a week later. Thankfully, little violence occurred in Providence, compared to many other cities in the country.

The next morning Governor John Chafee, who later in his career became Secretary of the Navy and then a U.S. Senator, entered the State

House on the way to his office on the second floor. He was a little awkward, not knowing quite how to approach us, and he asked "Why are all of you here?" I was sure that he knew that Dr. King had been assassinated, but was just unable to express himself to the group. He went up his office and a short while later he sent one of his aides down to the rotunda to bring me to his office. He expressed his feelings about Dr. King's death and his concern about what might happen in Providence. He asked if there was anything I needed and how long we planned to stay in the State House. I told him that I didn't know how long we would stay. He also asked what he could do to make it more comfortable for us since we were sleeping on marble floors. He said that he wanted to make the situation as comfortable for us as he could and would make sure that we had food and water. Then he asked me if I would be going out into the community to speak anywhere. At that point I had two engagements to speak–one at Brown University and the other on the Jack Comley television show. So Governor Chafee gave me the use of his limousine to get around that week.

Jack Comley was one of Rhode Island's media stars, and I had been on his radio and television shows before. I knew him and had a lot of respect for him. I appeared on Jack's show that day and we talked about Dr. King, about what had happened, and what was happening across the country. Jack was sympathetic to the Movement and expressed his feelings that day on the show. I don't recall exactly what he said, but it caused some anger in certain sections of the white community. Jack lived in the upscale community of Barrington, Rhode Island, and because of this program, his home was fire-bombed. Until his death a few years ago, Jack would always joke with me, saying, "I almost got my house burned down because of you!" Jack was not only a good broadcaster, but he was a good man as well.

Ralph and Coretta had gone to Memphis to pick up Martin's body and bring it back to Atlanta. They led a huge march through the city of Memphis. I hadn't gone to Atlanta, but had stayed in Providence immediately after the assassination, because I felt I would be more useful in Rhode Island and Massachusetts, where I could keep watch over the situation there. We planned to hold a rally at the State House that Sunday. I would speak at the rally and then immediately fly off to Atlanta for Martin's funeral. It was probably one of the largest rallies ever held in Providence. I know that it was the largest crowd that I had ever spoken to before. Several thousand people gathered on the State House lawn. There were half a dozen speakers, but I was the first speaker on the program so that I could leave and catch a plane. Governor Chafee's state trooper/driver drove me to the airport.

By the time I arrived in Atlanta and made my way to Ebenezer Baptist Church, the service had begun. Ralph was to do the eulogy with some assistance from Jesse Jackson. Thousands of people lined Auburn Avenue. I knew that the church would be full. Since the service had started, I decided not to enter the church, even though I knew I could have gotten in since the staff was to serve as pall bearers. I was still emotional from the speech I had given that morning back in Rhode Island, and I wasn't sure how I would hold up if I went into the church and saw Mrs. King and the children sitting there. I knew how much I was hurting, and I could only imagine the pain that they must have been feeling at that moment. Instead, I stayed outside where speakers had been set up so that people could listen to the service.

When the service was over and the staff brought the casket out of the church, I joined them and we lifted Martin's body onto a wagon, which was to be pulled to the cemetery by four mules. It was there at that moment that I said my goodbye to this wonderful man, my leader. Standing there by the wagon, I thought of how much I loved him and how much I would miss him.

We began to line people up to march in the procession as we waited for Ralph and Mrs. King and her family to leave the church. Once they came out, we moved the wagon up so they could take their positions in front of the procession, and the staff assembled around the wagon. I greeted Bernard Lee, who had been Martin's assistant since Montgomery. I knew how painful this must have been for him, and I gave him a hug. I nodded to Mrs. King, not knowing what to say to her in that moment, not knowing how to respond to her pain. I was afraid that if I said something to her right then, I would start to cry. And I did not want to cause her to break down. I knew that I would have the opportunity to speak with her later, so I turned and walked away. But as I walked away from the wagon, I began to cry. I don't know who it was, but someone put their arms around me. And as Hosea Williams, who was in front of the mules, began to lead them to begin the procession, I walked back to the wagon with this person's arm still around me.

Although Dr. King was later buried near the Martin Luther King Center for Social Change next to Ebenezer Baptist Church in Atlanta, originally he was buried more than five miles outside the city, so the procession that day was a long one. Thousands of people lined both sides of the road. As we passed Morehouse College, where Martin had received his Bachelor's degree at the age of nineteen, several hundred people were lined up. Throughout the procession, people were respectful; all had come to express their grief and their love for Dr. King. I was walking up front with Hosea in front of the mules when he suggested that the staff form a line between the crowds and Mrs. King and Ralph so they could have a little privacy.

Once we had formed this line, I looked over at the children and marveled at how composed they had been from the time they entered the church until now, during this very long walk. As we walked along, I remembered a conversation I once had with Martin about his children. He said that I had been so loyal to him that he trusted me to watch out for his children. At that moment Fred Bennett, who had gone to college with Martin, and who was walking in front with Ralph and Mrs. King, seemed to have the same thought as I did. We both moved towards the children.

Fred grabbed Martin III's hand, and I grabbed Yolanda's. We pulled the two of them and their brother Dexter out of the procession so they could walk more freely with us and could talk to each other. Bernice had been walking by her mother's side and didn't want to leave her at first. But when Andy saw what Fred and I had done with the oldest three, he walked over to Bernice and lifted her into his arms. As we walked along, it was for us a symbolic commitment to the children. They knew that Uncle Ralph, as they called him, would be there for them, and that Andy would be there as well. But now they knew that the rest of us would also be there if they needed us. As we proceeded towards the cemetery, we took turns carrying Bernice.

A number of celebrities attended the funeral, including Harry Belafonte and Sidney Poitier. Some stayed for a few days after the funeral. Some, such as Diana Ross and Joan Baez, stayed and greeted Ralph at his church. Joan and two other folk singers, Kirk Kilpatrick and James Cotton, stayed to perform for us during the following days as we gathered together to make decisions about SCLC's future. Kilpatrick stayed on to work for SCLC as a staff member, and he was one of the primary performers at Resurrection City.

During the days immediately after the funeral, some decisions had to be made. Would we go on with the Poor People's Campaign in the way that we originally planned, or would there be some changes, perhaps scaling down our plans? The other major decision, however, was who would lead SCLC. It was fairly clear that Ralph should be the leader, because that was what Martin had wanted. He had made it very clear that Ralph should succeed him, not only verbally but written into the policies of the board. But still there were questions, both outside of the organization and within SCLC itself. Some were suggesting that perhaps Jesse should be the leader because of his charisma. I disagreed since Jesse was one of the more recent staff members to come on board. If Ralph was not to be the leader, then I felt it should be someone who had been with SCLC longer than Jesse. My preference in that case would be Andy Young or Hosea Williams. But I felt strongly that Ralph deserved the role. He had been with Martin from the very beginning, and he cared deeply about SCLC. But the staff had to formalize the decision.

We gathered at Ralph's church, the West Hunter Street Baptist Church, to talk about these issues and make a decision about where to go from here and who would lead us there. All of us were still in pain and shock over the loss of Martin. But the first decision that had to be made was whether to go on with the Poor People's Campaign. Clearly, Ralph wanted to go on. And most of the staff wanted to go on as well because we felt we owed it to Martin to carry out his last vision. After much discussion, with everyone having a chance to give their input, we decided that we would proceed with the Poor People's Campaign as it was originally conceived by Martin.

The next issue was whether Ralph was going to lead us. After some discussion about Ralph's strengths and weaknesses, almost all of us agreed that he should succeed Martin as President of SCLC. We all committed ourselves to supporting Ralph and pledged that we would be with him, especially as we began the Poor People's Campaign into Washington. We wanted Ralph to know that we would walk with him as we had walked with Martin.

We all agreed that we would stay with SCLC, that none of us would leave at this point. We felt that we had to show Ralph and the world that we were together. Some of us, perhaps, would have liked to leave because of the pain that we were in, a pain that would not soon leave many of us. It was decided that those of us in the field should take a few days off to grieve, and then return to our assigned areas and await a decision about the new timetable for the campaign. Ralph and the executive staff were to begin immediate discussions about the Poor People's Campaign.

After I left the meeting and began walking over to the SCLC office, I thought back to the very first time I had laid eyes on Martin in the middle of Ebenezer Baptist Church, as I nervously waited to be interviewed by him. I remembered his smile and that wonderful laugh of his. What a beautiful man he was! I thought back to the time I was downstairs in the basement of the SCLC office when Dora called down and said that Dr. King wanted to see me. He wanted me to drive him to the YMCA. Although it was not far, he couldn't easily walk there because he would be stopped by everyone along the route. I thought back to playing softball with him; he was always the pitcher, while I played third base or right field. I thought back to the times I sat around his kitchen table sharing a meal with him. Sometimes it was just the two of us; other times, the kids would join us. All of these moments I will carry with me always, but I knew that I would never have an opportunity again to spend time with him. He was gone. He had been taken from me. But I was so grateful that God had put him in my life, even for a little while.

I thought of Martin and Ralph walking out on the balcony together on that fateful day in Memphis, and I imagined that the words to his favorite hymn might have run through his mind in those last moments:

"Precious Lord, take my hand
Lead me on, let me stand
I am tired, I am weak, I am worn
Through the storm, through the night
Lead me on to the light
Take my hand, precious Lord, lead me home."

When the darkness appears
And the night draws near
And the day is past and gone
At the river I stand
Guide my feet, hold my hand
Take my hand, precious Lord, lead me home."

The Poor People's Campaign

I returned to Providence from Atlanta and continued my preparations for the Poor People's Campaign. The delay had given me an opportunity to reach more people and put more things in place. Working in Providence and Boston, I focused on organizing a cross section of people to go to Washington. I was looking for families, single women heads-of-household, white and black poor people. Although I was trying to find people willing to go to Washington and stay for the duration, I was looking for people to go for a shorter period of time as well. I also needed people who would visit Resurrection City over the weekends; they would be the ones to deliver supplies for my contingent.

After Dr. King's funeral, when the decision was made to move forward with the campaign, I had asked Ralph if he would come to New England to help raise the issue of poverty there. Ralph was speaking around the country, and he agreed to come. I scheduled a time for him to spend two days in the area and organized two busloads of poor people to greet Ralph and his assistant, Bernard Lee, at Green Airport in Providence. Bernard Lee had served as assistant to Martin before his death and had traveled everywhere with him. Other than Ralph, he had known Martin longer than anyone else in SCLC. I felt that Bernard never really recovered from the shock of Martin's death, and he was one of the first SCLC staff members to pass away. He died of heart failure at the age of fifty-five.

In those days, airports had few security restrictions and people could go to the gate to meet arrivals. About seventy people marched with me through the terminal, and we welcomed Ralph with singing and cheering as he came through the gate. Many of these people were welfare mothers and members of the National Welfare Rights Organization, an organization founded by George Wiley, a native of Rhode Island.

After we left the airport, we went to the Pond Street Baptist Church where I had set up headquarters. Ralph, Bernard Lee, and I held a news conference and then marched through the streets of South Providence with about 500 people. We marched to the Providence City Hall where Ralph and I submitted a list of demands to the mayor, Joseph A. Doorley, Jr. These demands centered on employment, housing, education, and the elimination of poverty. We then met with Governor John Chafee to discuss these same issues. While Ralph was in town, we had a mass meeting at Saints Peter and Paul Cathedral, one of the largest facilities in Providence at that time that we could use at no cost. Before leaving, Ralph attended a reception/fundraiser at the home of Allan and Roberta Shine on the East Side, one of the most liberal and wealthy sections of the city.

One of the decisions made by the SCLC executive committee was for a small group to go to Washington before the people arrived and moved into Resurrection City. One hundred people from across the country, representing the make-up of the people who would be living there, would accompany Ralph. The group was called the Committee of One Hundred. I was asked to come and bring two people with me; I chose one person from Boston and one from Providence. We arrived in Washington the day before Ralph got there. Other representatives from the SCLC staff included Bernard Lee, J. T. Johnson, Walter Fauntroy, who was in charge of the Washington office, and Bob Green, Executive Director of SCLC at the time. A group from Philadelphia who was to provide security at Resurrection City also came.

On April 29, we marched from northwest Washington to the Capitol where Ralph and a number of the Committee of One Hundred testified before Congress. They presented to different congressional committees a list of ninety-nine demands, having to do with the conditions of poor people across the country. We also went to government departments, such as Agriculture, HUD, and Labor, to give testimony and present our concerns and demands for changes that would improve the quality of life for poor people. At one meeting, a white woman raised in Alabama said that she would not be tricked any longer into hating black people. This testimony represented the coming together that Dr. King had hoped for. We repeated this several times over a three-day period. After the three days, members of the Committee of One Hundred returned home to finish preparing their contingents for Resurrection City. I went back to New England, and Ralph went on to rally and mobilize people in the South.

We were getting close to the time when caravans from around the country would be heading to Washington, D.C. I began to focus on final preparations, arranging for buses and for the use of the Cranston Armory where people would gather to leave for Washington. James Orange came from time to time to help me out, since I was working in two cities. The caravan was to start in Marks, Mississippi, since that was Martin and Ralph's original plan, but there would now be a slight detour. Some of the southern leg of the caravan would go to Memphis to pay tribute to Dr. King and march through the city of Memphis. Then they would proceed to Marks. Ralph would drive the mule train as it left Marks.

In the meantime I was getting the Northeast caravan ready to go. By then, it was the Northeast caravan since we wound up getting several families from New Hampshire. The New Hampshire/Boston contingent arrived in Providence on three buses and went to the Cranston Street Armory where we had arranged for cots and food to be brought in. We also had milk and toys for the children. The contingent from Providence joined them at the Armory. People would be staying there for a couple nights while we got everything together and were ready to leave. James Orange and I made the final preparations before we headed out for Washington.

It was during this time that I learned more about the media and began to understand what it must be like for celebrities. In my earlier experiences with SCLC, I had tried to avoid the media. But here, I was in the news because I was promoting the Poor People's Campaign. I was being interviewed on television and radio, and articles were appearing in Rhode Island's largest newspaper, *The Providence Journal*. I was being identified by the media as a leader, not only of the Poor People's Campaign, but more specifically, as the "black leader" in Rhode Island. One of the problems in being identified as a "leader" by the media is that you sometimes get credit for things you don't really have anything to do with. I had been out of town when Freeman Soares, one of the local leaders, had organized a demonstration. When I got back, I showed up to support the march, but that night I was given credit for organizing the march. Since Freeman had organized the demonstration, this put a strain on our relationship and our ability to work together. Another aspect of being seen frequently in the media is that people know you, but you don't know them, which can be awkward when meeting people.

The media had been important in spreading the word about the Poor People's Campaign, and it would be important in telling the story once we arrived at Resurrection City. John Sweeney, who later went on to work for CNN, was a local TV reporter for WJAR-Channel 10 at the time and traveled with us to Resurrection City. Reporters from *The Providence Journal* also traveled with us, and they did a series on some of the people in our contingent while in Resurrection City.

It was early May when we finally pulled our caravan of seven buses and several cars and trucks from the Cranston Street Armory and onto Interstate 95 South heading towards Washington. Our first major stop was Philadelphia, where Ralph gave what I believe was one of his best speeches. He spoke before thousands at one of the largest outdoor parks in Philadelphia. We had made arrangements to stay at schools and other government facilities during our stops. We stayed in Philadelphia for a couple of days, and the contingent from Philadelphia and surrounding areas joined our caravan.

Our next stop was Montgomery County, Maryland, one of the richest areas in the country. John Sweeney often teased me about our choosing this spot to bring a large contingent of poor people. He had seen the reaction of some of the people in Montgomery County to our being there. But we had done this for a reason. We wanted to raise the consciousness of people to the plight of the poor. We wanted people to see the faces of the poor, to see who they were and to hear their stories. We stayed in Montgomery County for a couple days, our last stop before we reached D.C. and Resurrection City.

Resurrection City was located on the Mall between the Lincoln and Washington monuments. Ralph led the southern leg of the caravan to Resurrection City, and he arrived on May 13, leading the mule train to the site. He was accompanied by Hosea Williams and A. D. King, Martin's brother. James Orange, a couple other staff members and I led the New England contingent and met Ralph at Resurrection City. Once Ralph arrived, he drove the first stake into the ground to begin the building of

Resurrection City. I was standing near Ralph and watched as the Reverend Al Sampson held the stake and Ralph drove it into the ground. I looked at A. D. King and thought about Martin, wishing that he was there to share this moment with us—the fulfillment of his vision of bringing poor people together, living and working in Resurrection City.

Resurrection City

That was the beginning of Resurrection City. Once the caravans from the West and Midwest arrived to join the contingents from the South and the East, a total of five thousand people were ready to move into their new homes on the National Mall, where they would live for the next forty days. The Southern contingent included construction workers who, immediately upon their arrival, began to build housing for the new residents. The buildings were constructed of plywood and were different sizes. The larger ones were assigned to families and the smaller ones to single people. Resurrection City was not a place of comfort; it represented the way many people lived their lives.

The idea was that Resurrection City would be a peaceful, non-violent place, representing Dr. King's philosophy, but regrettably, it was not always the ideal place he had envisioned. There were bound to be problems because we had not transformed people's lives, and they had brought their issues with them. People who lived in the ghetto brought that environment to Resurrection City. We had problems with gangs, rapes, alcohol, and drugs. We had tried to prepare people and keep these things out of Resurrection City. But I think that in some ways we were naïve to believe that we could bring that many people together in one place and that they would leave the reality of their lives back in the ghetto, the barrios, or wherever they came from.

There were numerous other problems in Resurrection City. One major problem was the weather, which made rough conditions even more difficult. I think it rained more during that period in 1968 in Washington, D.C. than at any other time. We estimated that it rained more than thirty of the forty days we were there. For a good part of the time, we were in mud up above our ankles. Mud was everywhere. Given the conditions, I was assigned to the most difficult job in Resurrection City. I was in charge of sanitation and health.

We had a number of volunteers. People came from across the country to help us, and given the weather conditions, we needed that help. During storms we often lost power, and volunteer electricians would work throughout the night to keep the lights on. In addition to the volunteers, we also had people from the city and the Federal Government who were assigned to Resurrection City as a part of their official duties. The city assigned people from the Health Department, including a dietician. We provided and cooked our own food, so it was important that our food supply be safe. Catholic nuns came in almost every day to help prepare and serve the meals. Several workers from the City's Health and Sanitation Departments volunteered to work on my team at night after they had carried out their official duties.

We held demonstrations almost every day. Most of those demonstrations were targeted at specific departments–for example, the Agriculture Department, the Interior Department, or Capitol Hill itself. Ralph or other staff members, including myself, would lead some of the demonstrations. I helped lead two or three demonstrations with Native American chiefs to the Interior Department. The Interior Department was important to them in their effort to improve conditions on reservations and to gain recognition through the Bureau of Indian Affairs. We also demonstrated at the Supreme Court so that the Native Americans could submit petitions concerning the issue of fishing rights. They felt that the water and the land were theirs, given by God, so they should be able to fish wherever they liked. We demonstrated at the State Department where people raised the issue of the Vietnam War. We met with Secretary of State Dean Rusk, and one woman asked "Why should our sons die in Asia when our families lack freedom at home?"

During our many demonstrations, hundreds of people were arrested. I was arrested a couple of times during the early stages, before I had been assigned my responsibility for sanitation and health in Resurrection City.

After that, although I continued to lead or participate in demonstrations, it was felt that I was more valuable in Resurrection City than in jail. Members of the Gutherz family marched with me on several occasions. Ralph spent more than half the time we were in Resurrection City in jail. Hosea Williams was with him most of that time, and became his jail partner.

Some of the issues within SCLC began to surface. The conflict between Hosea Williams and Jesse Jackson soon became obvious to everyone. Ralph had appointed Hosea to be the Mayor of Resurrection City, but Jesse wanted the title. This was clear to everyone in Resurrection City, because whenever Hosea would say something, Jesse tried to counter it. Unfortunately, Ralph allowed this to go on too long, and the conflict between Jesse and Hosea caused discord within Resurrection City, and outside as well. The level of coordination that was usually a part of SCLC's activities did not exist. For example, from time to time without any real preparation, Jesse would get on the PA system and announce that he was going to lead a demonstration. Jesse would lead a demonstration on one department, and Hosea would lead one on another. Such competitiveness made it difficult for the residents, who had to decide whether to follow Jesse or Hosea. Then there were times when Ralph would lead marches as well. The situation began to raise questions about Ralph's leadership. Some felt that he should be the one to lead most of the demonstrations, or that he should have assigned people to lead the demonstrations, rather than their doing it on an ad hoc basis. Another area of conflict was that Ralph and some of the other SCLC staff stayed many nights at a hotel, instead of sleeping in Resurrection City.

Another problem for SCLC staff concerned A.D. King. A.D. was drinking heavily at the time, and it was difficult trying to keep him under wraps, both from the residents of Resurrection City, but even more important from the media. A.D. perhaps suffered more than anyone at the loss of Martin, even though in some ways Ralph had more of a brotherly relationship with him. It's not that Martin and A.D. were not close, but Ralph had spent more time with Martin in recent years, and they had developed an extraordinary relationship. Sadly, a year or two later, A.D. was found dead in his swimming pool.

I had prepared quite well for my New England contingent. I had made arrangements for supplies to be delivered, and I went back to Providence a couple times to pick up money that had been collected. But as we went on with Resurrection City, it became clear that SCLC hadn't prepared for any kind of educational program or enough activities for the children, perhaps because it was summer. But I felt that it was important for the children that I brought to Resurrection City to receive some sort of education or tutorial program to keep them occupied while their parents were off demonstrating in various parts of D.C. I called upon the Gutherz family to help me out in providing some services for my contingent.

The Gutherz responded to my call, and the entire family came to D.C. They trampled through the mud like those of us who were living in Resurrection City. They helped me set up a school so that the children would have some kind of educational program. Even more important, they made sure there were activities and games to occupy the young people while their parents were off marching on the Agriculture Department and the Health Department. They set up a bakery so there would be a useful activity for the children. The Gutherz came and they went to work. Not only did they go to work, but they trained people to keep everything going when they had to leave. These activities were not available just to the New England contingent. Helene made sure that all of the children at Resurrection City could come and participate in what they were doing. This is just one instance of how the Gutherz family responded to my calls for assistance while I was in the Movement. A little over a year later they would respond once again when I was reassigned to Ridgeville, South Carolina.

We began to lose control over some of the gangs that had come to Resurrection City with us from Chicago, Philadelphia, and other large cities. We had felt that we would be able to control these gangs, since staff had worked with them for a long period of time to provide discipline and make them aware of non-violence. One reason for including them was to get them off the streets of the urban cities and make them more productive–to get them involved in something larger than themselves. But after awhile in Resurrection City, these gang members had too much time on their hands and began to slip back into their bad habits. One Saturday night while the soul singer, Billy Stewart, was performing, some of the gang members started taunting the D.C. police officers at the perimeter of Resurrection City. I don't know exactly what they were doing, but I believe that, besides taunting the police officers, they were throwing things at passing cars. The police responded by lobbing tear gas into Resurrection City.

I was choking from the tear gas as I ran with some of my staff back to our camp to help them deal with the thick cloud of tear gas. I ordered them to run to the rear of Resurrection City and head for the Washington Monument. I knew that we needed to get the children out of Resurrection City, because the gas would last for a while and some of the children could become very sick. We sat out on the Mall for a couple hours to allow the gas to dissipate before we re-entered. The police did not interfere with us because they understood that people needed to get out of Resurrection City to escape the tear gas. Because of this incident, Ralph and Andy grew increasingly concerned about how to deal with the gang members. The particular group that caused this problem was asked to leave.

Another problem had surfaced as well. An outside group had volunteered to provide security for Resurrection City and also for Ralph. This group was not a professional security force, but in the past we had occasionally used this same type of security for Martin and Ralph with few problems. However, one of the difficulties in Washington was that Ralph to some degree was being kept from the residents of Resurrection City, as well as from staff, by the security group. Perhaps they were overly cautious because of Dr. King's recent assassination, but Ralph was not as accessible to people as he wanted or needed to be. When people tried to approach him, members of the security group would push them away. I understood the need for security at Resurrection City. There had to be some form of policing, although this went a little too far in terms of how staff and residents were being dealt with. Some people began to feel as though they were back on an urban street, dealing with city police. Ralph was uncomfortable with this approach as well and requested that they give him more room to communicate with people. The situation improved and, at least in Resurrection City, Ralph was given more freedom to walk around and talk with people.

My job was to try to keep Resurrection City as clean as possible and prevent any kind of outbreak of disease as a result of a lack of sanitation. I had to work with the residents to make sure that they were properly disposing of their garbage and that they were taking showers. I also had to work with D.C. officials to make sure that they came in periodically to check that everything was all right. I worked with companies to deal with restroom facilities, exterminators, and so forth. Most of the sanitation crew were volunteers from Resurrection City itself, but we had some volunteers from D.C. as well. We picked up trash two or three times a day. The constant rain, however, made it especially difficult to keep Resurrection City clean and healthy because of the ever-present mud.

Many entertainers and actors visited Resurrection City to perform, such as Lou Rawls, Eartha Kitt, Tony Bennett, Harry Belafonte, and others. And on Solidarity Day, there was a who's who of the entertainment world. Joan Baez, as usual, was often there and gave a good deal of her time and energy working with people. Also, I gained a great deal of respect for several actors and performers who didn't come just to entertain or sign a few autographs. They came to chip in, roll up their sleeves, and work. One who came and worked really hard was Robert Culp from the TV series, "I Spy."

When Robert Culp came to Resurrection City, he volunteered to be on the sanitation crew. For two weeks he picked up garbage, carried water, and unloaded supplies. He wasn't an actor during those two weeks. He was someone who cared about people and who wanted to support the Poor People's Campaign, not in a flashy way by making speeches and signing autographs, but by laboring like the residents of Resurrection City and like the garbage workers in Memphis that Dr. King gave his life supporting.

Entertainers supported SCLC almost from the beginning. Two who had supported SCLC since Montgomery and Selma were Harry Belafonte and Sammy Davis, Jr. Harry Belafonte especially liked being with the people at Resurrection City, and he volunteered for a number of jobs, including working in my area picking up garbage. I admired both Harry Belafonte and Robert Culp, because they cared about people and didn't mind getting their hands dirty working beside them.

We had some supporters who lived in D.C. These people brought supplies and allowed some of us to use their homes to take warm showers and wash the mud from our clothes. Some merchants in the business community donated clothing and shoes. A few members of Congress supported us, even when we were marching on Capitol Hill and even on the day we attempted to take over the Capitol grounds for a picnic and many were arrested. George McGovern, Eugene McCarthy, and a few others, came to Resurrection City as a way of showing support for our efforts.

Two special events took place in Resurrection City. Both were moving, and I was glad to be a witness to them. The first was an event on June 19 that we called Solidarity Day. We had put out a call to the entire country, asking people to come to Washington and support us. More than 100,000 people came. In addition to the people from around the nation, major entertainers were there. It was the largest audience that Ralph had ever spoken to, and it was an important speech for him. But even on that special day, Jesse Jackson and James Bevel did not give Ralph the respect that he deserved. Andy finally told them to leave Ralph alone, that this was a big day for him.

I was happy to be there that day as an SCLC staff member, especially to be standing in front of the Lincoln Memorial where thousands had stood in 1963 to hear Martin Luther King, Jr. deliver his famous speech. I wasn't at that gathering, but I was there for Solidarity Day and witnessed Coretta Scott King and Ralph David Abernathy giving their speeches before thousands. Poor people and their supporters were coming together– coming together in solidarity. I hoped that something would come from our efforts, that something would come from the people who had traveled to Resurrection City from all over the nation, and that the nation would see the faces of the poor and hear their voices. I also hoped that after seeing and hearing Ralph, the nation might view him in a new light, out from the shadow of Martin, and I hoped that they would listen to this new voice. Solidarity Day was important. It held up the plight of the poor before the conscience of America.

The other event at Resurrection City had come before Solidarity Day, after another tragedy, another assassination. Martin had been dead only a couple of months when Robert Kennedy was assassinated in Los Angeles on June 5. When people in Resurrection City heard the news late that night, they became very upset and angry. They had lost another leader. People had put their hopes in Robert Kennedy. He and George McGovern had been instrumental in raising the plight of the poor. Kennedy and McGovern had gone to Mississippi and witnessed the poverty and the hunger there. They had supported Martin's vision of the Poor People's Campaign. Many of the residents of Resurrection City began to act out their anger. Some of that anger spilled outside of Resurrection City itself, and there was a confrontation between police and residents. Once again police used tear gas to stop those outside of Resurrection City, but the tear gas drifted into the City, causing problems for some of the residents.

After the assassination, Kennedy's body was carried across the country on a train. When the train arrived in Washington, D.C., his body was loaded on a hearse, which headed for Resurrection City. I will never forget the moment that the hearse made its loop from behind the Lincoln Memorial. I stood with almost all the residents of Resurrection City as the hearse moved slowly by. I stood on the curb and said goodbye to the man who had done so much to give a voice to the poor. Resurrection City had not been so quiet since it was erected. It was stone silent. That was a powerful moment that I will carry with me always.

But it took me back to April 4 when I said goodbye to Martin in a different way. Maybe I hadn't grieved in the way that I needed to grieve for Martin because I was so busy carrying out his last campaign. But when Robert Kennedy came to Resurrection City for the last time, I grieved for him and for Martin. I understood that without the two of them, the road would be long and it would be hard. With the two of them speaking out, America had seemed on the verge of change. But madness and violence had now taken them both.

I will remember all of the events of D.C. and Resurrection City. I will remember the marches, the jail, and the mud. But these two events–Solidarity Day and saying goodbye to Robert Kennedy–stand out the most.

The Poor People's Campaign was an important campaign in many ways. It was important because it was Martin's vision. It was important that the plight of the poor be put on center stage. It was important that the voices of the poor be heard and for them to be able to speak for themselves. But it was becoming clear that our efforts would not be successful and that we would leave with little more than what we came with, because we had been unable to get Congress to commit to any legislation that would change the plight of the poor. I knew that we would have to fight this battle again somewhere else, at some other time. On the positive side, however, for the first time poor people had had the opportunity to come together. Red, white, black, and brown people had come together with a common goal.

We had planted the seed through the Poor People's Campaign, and the government did pay heed to the concerns raised by the people of Resurrection City. After we had packed up, left Washington, and returned home, we began to see some changes. The government began to invest in nutrition programs. Food stamps became more widely available, and they provided for more than the once a month commodity program through the Agriculture Department. School lunches became more accessible to poor children all over the country, and children no longer had to go off to school hungry and come home hungry. The school lunch program helped many families survive. The Poor People's Campaign was a struggle, and circumstances were difficult for those who had come to live in Resurrection City. But the Poor People's Campaign was not in vain.

Some of the contingents began to leave Resurrection City and travel back home to resume their normal life—return to their cities, to their reservations, to their barrios, to their ghettos. The weeks had been long for all of us. The rain and the mud were beginning to take their toll. For me, it had been a long struggle. My responsibilities were weighing heavily on my shoulders. In some ways, I felt that I had more responsibility than even Ralph or Andy, because it fell upon me to keep Resurrection City clean and the inhabitants healthy. Meanwhile, the pressure from Washington, D.C. was intensifying. We had stayed beyond the time that our permit allowed us to stay on the Mall, and the government was beginning to come down on us. Conditions were deteriorating, and they were concerned about safety issues. They wanted us to leave the Mall.

In all of the campaigns I had been involved in as an SCLC staff member, I always wanted to fight to the end to make sure that we could claim some sort of victory and give people something to feel good about. But this was one time that I was willing to take our loss and move on. The city of Washington had set a new deadline for us to leave. Soon our numbers had dwindled down from thousands to a few hundred. Jesse had gone back to Chicago. Bernard Lafayette had gone back to Atlanta. And other staff members were leading their contingents back home. I had to prepare my contingent to go back to New England, although I would not be going back with them. I needed to be there until the end. It made no sense at this stage for another SCLC staff member to take on my responsibility as Sanitation Director since I had established a good working relationship with the city, the Federal Government, and the contractors. I had volunteers working with me who were capable of getting my contingent back safely, with the exception of a few families who had decided to stay with me.

As the deadline approached, we had to decide how we would leave

Resurrection City. Would people just pick up their belongings and go their separate ways? Or would most of us leave together? Ralph made the decision that he wanted to make one last stand. He wanted to lead the people out of Resurrection City once again. The officials had told us that if we hadn't left by a certain time, all of those who remained in Resurrection City would be arrested. They informed us that the police would mass around 7:00 a.m. to evict us.

On that day Ralph left his hotel room early so that he would be at Resurrection City when the police arrived. We had separated the more than 200 people who would follow Ralph from the fifty or so of us who would remain in Washington, D.C. The smaller group moved out of Resurrection City before the police arrived that morning but stood on the sidewalk. The larger group that would be going to jail with Ralph stayed with him in Resurrection City. I stayed as well but moved off to the side so that I could deal with the officials after the group had been arrested. Ralph gathered together those people who would be following him on this last journey out of Resurrection City and began to pray. The police began to move into Resurrection City, and Ralph led his small band towards them. As they met, Ralph said a few words and then two officers on either side of Ralph led him and the others out of Resurrection City into paddy wagons.

As I stood off to the side watching the paddy wagons move away, I was approached by the Director of the Health Department, asking if I had prepared everything else to be taken away. I responded that Resurrection City was ready to be handed over. He then gave the order for the workmen to move into Resurrection City. The bulldozers moved in from the 17th Street entrance and began knocking down the structures that we had built weeks before. I watched as the buildings collapsed. Soon there was no more Resurrection City. By the end of the day, it looked as if we had never been there.

A wooden sign left behind by someone expressed the feelings of the residents of Resurrection City:

> "We came in droves with new hope
> The young–The old–The gritty.
> We dared to build upon a dream
> in Resurrection City.

We left behind hopelessness
for we were tired of pity.
We seek only true dignity."

It ended almost as it had begun. I had been one of the first staff members to come to Washington before the Committee of One Hundred arrived, and now I would be one of the last to leave. Walter Fauntroy and I were left behind to deal with the city and the government about any issues that remained to be cleared up. Ralph and his group lingered behind jail bars for another couple of weeks. The smaller group that didn't go to jail wandered around Washington, D.C. It soon became clear to me that there was no longer a reason for Ralph to stay in jail, and there was no reason for the rest of us to be in Washington. It was time to go home. Walter communicated to Ralph that no purpose was being served by him remaining in jail. Ralph agreed and said that he would leave in a couple of days. The small group still in Washington met Ralph and the others as they left the jail. The day after we had put Ralph and Hosea on a plane to Atlanta, everyone began to disperse.

I got in a car and began to drive out of Washington. I drove down Rhode Island Avenue on the way to Interstate 95 North, heading for Providence. As I drove, I thought about Martin. I thought about all the hard work he had put into bringing about the Poor People's Campaign and that he hadn't been there with us in Resurrection City. I grew sad at the realization that I would never see him again, that he was really gone from me and from all of us. I felt that I had served him well in Resurrection City on this, his last vision. As I drove, I wondered what would be next. But I wouldn't worry about that now. Now I was just looking forward to sometime later that night finally being able to fall asleep in my own bed.

The Holy City

The city of Charleston has seen its share of battles, destruction from fires, hurricanes and even one of the most powerful earthquakes to hit the eastern United States. Charleston is where the first shot of the Civil War was fired, when Confederate forces fired cannons from the Battery at Union-occupied Fort Sumter in Charleston Harbor. Charleston is known as "The Holy City" because of its history of religious tolerance and because of its many churches. Church steeples dot the skyline of Charleston. It was the first Southern city to establish a Baptist church, just a few years after the First Baptist Church in America was established in Rhode Island in the late seventeenth century. And until the early nineteenth century, South Carolina had the largest Jewish population of any other state, with most living in Charleston.

Charleston also had an unusually large slave population in the eighteenth and nineteenth centuries. Many of the slaves worked in exhausting, unhealthy, and dangerous conditions on the rice plantations just outside the city. The Charleston area was the site of the Stono Rebellion, a slave revolt in 1739, and it is where one of the largest slave revolts in the United States would have taken place if in 1822, Denmark Vesey and other leaders had not been arrested and executed before it could begin. Charleston and its people, both black and white, have seen their share of hardship and conflict throughout the city's history. Today, Charleston, steeped in history, is a city of beautifully restored historic homes and buildings, with palmetto trees flanking its streets and moss-draped oaks gracing its parks. Charleston is a major tourist destination.

But in 1969, Charleston was facing another battle, a battle that was a legacy of its slave history, a battle that would impact the entire city, even the state of South Carolina. Workers at the two major hospitals in the City of Charleston–Charleston County Hospital and the Medical College–had gone on strike around the issues of better working conditions and higher wages. Most of the workers were black women who filled the lowest paid jobs: nurse's aides, practical nurses, technicians, and cafeteria workers. The workers had filed grievances, but when their concerns were not addressed, they decided to form a union. Charleston was anti-union, which is still true today, but was even more so in those days. As they attempted to organize, several of the workers at County Hospital were abruptly fired. When this happened, 450 other hospital workers walked off their jobs in protest, and then the workers at the Medical College followed suit.

The union they wanted to represent them was 1199-A, out of New York. This union represented textile workers and hotel workers in New York City, but now was attempting to organize hospital workers for the first time in one of the most anti-union states in the country. Once the workers walked off their jobs in protest, the situation escalated and it became a bigger conflict. The workers were not only in battle with the hospitals, but they were in battle with the city and the state. Normally, 1199-A would have requested support from other unions. However, most of these workers were black and poor, so rather than calling upon other unions for help, 1199-A reached out to a civil rights organization, the Southern Christian Leadership Conference, for help with this particular battle.

In some ways, Ralph needed a battle as well. He needed a battle that he could lead on his own. A battle that he could plan and execute himself; and not one that had been planned by Martin. So when he got the call from 1199-A, he thought that this might be a battle that he and SCLC could join. He sent James Orange to Charleston to assess the situation. When James reported back that it seemed to be something that SCLC could take on, Ralph made the decision that SCLC should support the hospital workers in their fight for dignity and decent wages. But before initiating any action in the city, Ralph went to Charleston to speak to the workers. Meanwhile SCLC staff members from around the country were reassigned to Charleston. I had been working in Providence, Rhode Island, since the end of the Poor People's Campaign in Washington, D.C. in 1968, and I was one of the staff reassigned.

One of the reasons that Ralph made the decision to support the hospital workers was because in some ways, it was a continuation of the Poor People's Campaign. Some of the issues raised during the Poor People's Campaign were similar to the issues of concern to the hospital workers, such as poor working conditions and low wages. One of the plans we had discussed in Washington was establishing Poor People's Embassies where we would bring several organizations together in one space and help coordinate a unified effort. I had been sent back to Rhode Island to continue this effort on a local level, and most SCLC staff had been sent back to their previous assignments to do the same. We had not been able to establish a Poor People's Embassy in Washington, D.C. and unfortunately we found it to be even more difficult to do it in the field. So, in some ways, the hospital workers gave SCLC a chance to do what we had set out to do during the Poor People's Campaign.

SCLC set up an office in the Brooks Hotel, a black-owned hotel on Morris Street at the edge of the black community. The hotel consisted of regular hotel rooms, a boarding house, and a restaurant across the street. SCLC took over several of the rooms as office space. When I arrived in Charleston, I was picked up at the airport and brought directly to the hotel. When I arrived at the office, Terrie Randolph was there. She arranged for my room and reimbursed me for my travel expenses to Charleston. She informed me that there would be a mass meeting that evening and then a staff meeting the following morning. She said I would be briefed at the staff meeting on the hospital workers themselves, their goals and objectives, as well as SCLC's role in supporting the workers and my overall assignment in this effort.

After I checked into my room and came back to the office, Andy Young greeted me. As Executive Vice-President, Andy was in charge of the staff, although it was the field directors that reported to him. About twenty staff had arrived in Charleston by this time, and we planned to pull additional staff from other projects as needed. There were projects currently underway in Mississippi and southwest Georgia under the direction of Hosea Williams. We had more national office staff in Charleston than we usually had on projects, but this was a significant campaign. Ralph returned to Atlanta to get a few days rest from the activities in Charleston and also to attend to some business at the national office.

At the mass meeting that evening at the Morris Brown AME Church, the main speakers were Mary Moultrie of the hospital workers and James Bevel of SCLC. Bevel was in charge of direct action, so he was the chief strategist for our efforts in Charleston and decided what tactics we would use in the campaign. Although we all had input, he had the ultimate responsibility as to how we would move forward in regards to a strategy. The church was full that night. Bevel informed people about the possibility of a night march before the week was over, a technique we had used throughout the South. I had used this technique when I first came to Providence to focus attention on the issue of fair housing, leading marches at night on Providence's East Side, the wealthiest section of the city. Having demonstrations at night had proven to be successful, but at the same time could be dangerous in terms of being able to see what was going on and anticipate what might happen. It wasn't as easy to keep people under control at night.

During marches, SCLC staff members were not usually in the midst of the other marchers or demonstrators. Normally, our role was to flank the demonstration. We walked on either side of the marchers, or in the front or rear, because we each had responsibility for keeping a certain number of marchers under control. We also had to keep other people from interfering with the marchers or breaking into line. This was particularly true if Martin or Ralph were leading the march. If the march took place at night, this was even more important. The first time that Martin and Ralph went to Memphis to lead a demonstration of the sanitation workers, there had been no staff preparation and no workshops for the people who were to march that day. No staff were on hand, and therefore there was no control by anyone trained to handle a march. People broke into the line from the rear, which ultimately led to the riots that occurred on that day in Memphis.

Now that SCLC staff had arrived, Ralph came back to Charleston to intensify the efforts being made in support of the hospital workers. Several busloads of people met him at the airport to welcome him back. In Charleston we began daily marches to the hospitals, sometimes more than one. Those participating were the workers from that particular hospital, although a few community people marched with them. We would occasionally allow young people in these marches, but usually, young people participated only in the daytime demonstrations away from the hospitals. We used community people, mostly adults, for the nighttime marches. Young people made up the bulk of the demonstrators when there were civil disobedience actions that we initiated or when we decided to go to jail. James Orange worked extremely hard training young people throughout the city, so they would be ready for the tactics that we put into place.

Ralph was eager to lead the first nighttime march. We wanted to see how the authorities would respond to this kind of direct action, which would be considered civil disobedience since there was a ban on nighttime demonstrations. Ralph led the march from the Morris Brown AME Church towards King Street. Although we were headed in the direction of downtown, we had decided that we would not go all the way into the business district. Instead we would march for about four blocks and then make a U-turn and return to the church. We were met at King Street by two or three police cars. The police officers did not try to interfere with the march even though we were banned from having a nighttime march. We made the U-turn as planned and headed back towards the church.

After a couple of blocks, we heard a sound away from the marchers that sounded like a pistol shot. The marchers reacted to what they thought was a shot, and seemed uncertain about what to do. I was responsible for controlling twenty-five people, and I kept them marching back to the church and did not let them break rank. Once I saw that they were under control, I moved to the rear of the march, along with some of the other staff, to make sure that nothing could occur there that we were unaware of. This tactic also let us see if extra police were responding to the incident. As usual, SCLC staff members were at the head of the march ahead of Ralph. In this case, it was James Orange and James Bevel, and they suggested to Ralph that we pick up the pace and get back to the church.

Ralph felt that the nighttime march had been successful, and most of us agreed. We had about 400 people marching and there had been no injuries or arrests. We had made our point that we would not be bound by the authorities' ban on nighttime marching or the curfew imposed by the governor. After we returned to the church, Ralph said a few words to those who had marched that night, and then Bevel talked about what would happen the next day. At our staff meeting the following morning, we talked about the march and began to discuss how we could intensify our civil disobedience as a part of the campaign. This march was the first of a series of nighttime marches led by the staff, including myself, who had experience leading nighttime marches prior to our effort in Charleston.

One evening a rally was scheduled at Morris Street Baptist Church, where Ralph was scheduled to speak. However, he, Andy Young, and James Bevel had gone to James Island for dinner at someone's home and were late getting back into the city. We delayed the rally for a while, hoping they would arrive. But as it got late, I decided to speak to the several hundred people attending the mass meeting myself, since I was one of the senior staff present. I spoke for about ten minutes and had gotten them to the point where they were ready to go into battle. I asked them if they were ready to hit the streets and march towards downtown. They shouted back, "We are ready!" So another staff member and I led people from the church towards downtown.

My goal that night was to see if we could get a little further into downtown without being arrested. Since no official decision had been made as to whether we should even march that night, I knew that we shouldn't get arrested. I made the decision that if the police confronted us, we would immediately turn around and return to the church. However, Ralph and Bevel finally caught up with us. I moved off to the left so that Ralph could take over leading the march. We had no problem during the march and returned to the church where Ralph apologized to the people for being late and not speaking as he had planned. At that moment Ralph seemed in a reflective mood, and he said that he was missing Martin. He called me to his side and said to the audience, "You can see by the depth of our organization that I don't always have to be here for action to take place." I was pleased that Ralph had acknowledged me and my leadership skills before the people of Charleston. It reinforced my own confidence in my abilities, and it let people know that they could accept what I said and follow me into battle.

The purpose of the demonstrations on the hospitals was primarily to put pressure on the hospital administrators and persuade them to recognize the union. But we were not only dealing with the local authorities; we were also dealing with Governor Robert McNair, who from the very beginning had put the National Guard on alert. It was clear to us that if we limited our efforts to marching on the hospitals, we would not be successful. We had to broaden the support from the community and put more pressure on the city of Charleston. If we put pressure on the business community, they, in turn, would put pressure on local and state officials. To do this, we would have to interrupt the normal flow of business. Charleston is a major convention spot for groups from around the country, and we had to make it uncomfortable for groups who wanted to hold their conventions or conferences in Charleston.

One of my assignments was to disrupt the flow of business. We did this by breaking down into hit-and-run teams. I was very comfortable leading this kind of direct action, for I had done it in other places. Civil disobedience was something I had been trained to do, and I knew I could control the situation. When hit-and-run teams were used, if one team was arrested, then another team would strike in another part of the city. In Charleston we did such things as going into hotels and department stores to interfere with the transactions taking place and make the people shopping downtown uncomfortable. I would lead a team of fifteen to twenty young people into the major department stores, with the young people dribbling basketballs and ringing cowbells. Several times a day we would go into a department store for a few minutes and then move on to another store.

Also, I led teams into the Francis Marion Hotel, at the time one of the best hotels in Charleston, and we marched around their lobby and made noise as a part of our civil disobedience. For some of the young people, this was the first time that they had set foot inside this grand hotel or any of the upscale stores downtown.

Another team that I led interrupted the flow of traffic. Young people blocked the major intersections downtown, such as King and Calhoun Streets, a major intersection leading to the heart of downtown. We also occasionally blocked the flow of traffic onto some of the bridges. We wanted things to come to a stop. We knew that in some of these instances we would be arrested, particularly true when we blocked traffic.

An increasing number of people were being arrested and sent to jail as we continued with these kinds of activities. The first time I was arrested in Charleston resulted from the interruption of traffic on lower King Street, the heart of the business district. I was leading about twenty young people in this effort, and we were all taken into custody. On the way to jail, we were singing and dancing so much that the paddy wagons were rocking. Even in our jail cells, we continued with this until we were finally released.

James Orange and I also led marches on the Battery every other day. The Battery is a prime area for tourists to visit since it is where the first shot of the Civil War rang out and it is also where most of the mansions in Charleston are located. Even though our intention was to bring our cause to the attention of the tourists, I found myself affected emotionally by this area. I was in awe of being in the place that divided the nation, ultimately ending slavery. But I was also aware that I was giving voice to those descendents of slaves who worked so hard to provide care for Charlestonians in their hospitals.

This was just the beginning of our civil disobedience and our disruption of business as usual in Charleston. But it was already having an impact on the business community and they were losing business daily. Also, conferences scheduled for Charleston were being cancelled because we were targeting the facilities where conferences were held. SCLC's national office was keeping track of the effect of our actions on businesses in Charleston. Also, we monitored the reports in *The Post and Courier*, Charleston's local newspaper, concerning this.

It was very important that we prepare the entire black community for the civil disobedience that we had begun, because we needed them to support this effort. We canvassed neighborhoods throughout the black community, talking to them about the civil disobedience and preparing them for the boycott that we were planning and the sacrifices that they would have to make to honor the boycott. The black church was crucial in this effort. They provided meeting space to hold our rallies and a place from which to stage our demonstrations. Without the support of the black church and the clergy, this task would have been much more difficult. We also reached out to the white churches, and we did get support from a few of them. Churches provided food items and financial support for the families of the hospital workers. We also had the support of organizations such as the NAACP, the Black Historical Society, and neighborhood groups.

We worked to involve the black professional middle class in our efforts. It was especially important that they not shop at downtown businesses when we declared a boycott of downtown Charleston. Although we needed the support of the entire community, it was important that the power structure see that black professionals were supporting this effort as well. Also, they were important as we continued our night marches. They would come to the mass meetings and march with us at night, which allowed the hospital workers a chance to rest for the following day.

In addition to a boycott of businesses, Ralph called for a boycott of schools. We began to pull children out of school in order to make use of their youthful energy in support of this campaign. We had used this method in Birmingham, and it had been very successful. As we prepared to intensify our effort in committing civil disobedience, young people would be the catalyst in that effort, and it would be the young people that would go to jail.

Charleston at this point was becoming an armed camp. Governor McNair had had the National Guard on the scene from the first day that Ralph led a march. There were large contingents of state police as well, basically under the direction of John Francis Conroy, Chief of Police in Charleston. The hospital strike lasted almost 140 days. During that time, there were many demonstrations in all parts of the community, with different staff and local people leading the demonstrations. Charleston was losing hundreds of thousands of dollars a day from lost revenue.

We decided to hold a massive march through the city of Charleston on Mother's Day. We felt that Mother's Day was an ideal time to put thousands of women into the street since most of the workers were women, and a sizable number were mothers. The morning before Mother's Day, Juanita Abernathy and Coretta Scott King flew in from Atlanta together, bringing with them some of the women staff members from the SCLC national office. Although Mrs. Abernathy and Mrs. King had each been to Charleston since the beginning of the strike, this would be their only joint appearance together. That Saturday morning a number of hospital workers and SCLC staff met them at the airport, and then some of us gathered at Septima Clark's home for a brunch. As I sat there, I wondered how many more times this group would gather like this since Mrs. King was now putting most of her efforts into the Center for Nonviolent Social Change.

Mrs. King was the biggest draw on the Mother's Day march. It had been just a little over a year since Martin had been assassinated, and I think people wanted to see how she was holding up. She, along with Ralph and Mrs. Abernathy, led the march. As we marched from the Charleston/ North Charleston line towards downtown, thousands of people lined both sides of the street, watching as we passed. We had brought people in from around the country, and more than twenty thousand people participated in the march. Some of the people who came included Walter Reuther of the Auto Workers Union, Bill Kircher of the AFL/CIO, and congressmen such as John Conyers and Charles Dingham. This Mother's Day march would be the largest march that Ralph had led.

After the Mother's Day march, Ralph spent a significant amount of time in jail. On two occasions, he spent two weeks or more locked up. We were putting hundreds of people in jail each day, and the jails had reached their capacity. Both the county and city jails were full, so the authorities had to look for other places to hold people. It was during this period that Ralph appealed to the white churches in Charleston. He wrote an open letter to the community, similar to the letter Martin had written in Birmingham back in 1963. We distributed the letter on a Friday morning to most of the churches in the city, white as well as black. We hoped that pastors, as they put the finishing touches on their sermons, might use portions of Ralph's letter in their sermons on Sunday. *The Post and Courier* also printed excerpts from the letter. I don't know what the reaction was in the white churches, but it was fairly well received in the black churches.

Also, like Martin in Birmingham, Ralph was refusing to leave jail. One of the differences this time, however, was that Ralph didn't have a jail partner, which was not customary for SCLC. Although Andy was in Charleston, SCLC did not allow him to go to jail. Andy was SCLC's major negotiator, and it was always important that he remain out of jail so he could talk to officials. This had been the case from the beginning when he first joined SCLC. Hosea Williams had been working mostly in Mississippi and Atlanta during the Charleston campaign, although he had come to speak a couple of times. This time, however, Hosea came to Charleston in order to be Ralph's jail partner, and he stayed in jail with him until a tentative agreement to end the strike had been reached. Only then did the two of them leave jail, along with the hundreds of others who had been jailed with them.

Ralph was a little disappointed with the tentative agreement that had been reached between the workers and the hospital, and wondered if he had come out of jail too soon. But he wasn't sure it would be possible for him to go back to jail, given the tentative agreement. He felt that the increase in wages that the workers would be getting with this agreement was not as good as it should be. But the issue for the workers was their recognition, the re-hiring of those who had been fired, and their dignity. As in most of our campaigns, it was the local leaders who made the ultimate decisions about what was successful. But in spite of that, Ralph decided to send Andy back to the negotiating table to see if the agreement could be enhanced since the business community was clearly putting pressure on the hospitals and the governor.

Because of that decision, our actions in Charleston had an impact on the larger black community and on people outside of Charleston. One of the final results of the negotiations was that the black community would receive better healthcare. Some of the doctors felt that the hospital wasn't allowing them to provide the kind of service that they would like to provide; the final agreement gave them more freedom to serve the community. This was particularly true for the Medical College. Another result was that more than 120,000 state workers in South Carolina also received higher wages. Ralph was satisfied with the final agreement because it was more in line with our efforts in the Poor People's Campaign to redistribute the wealth. He was willing to sign off on it and to consider the Charleston campaign a victory.

While Ralph and Hosea were in jail, I began to have mixed feelings about SCLC staff. Signs of the stress resulting from Martin's death were still lingering. Most of us hadn't had a break since Martin's death, since we had immediately begun to push forward with the Poor People's Campaign. Some staff began showing signs of some of the demons that they had been able to push aside while in the Movement, such as heavy drinking, violent confrontations, and so forth. These types of behavior made me wonder how long we could be as effective as we had been in Charleston and what was going to happen to us.

There had also been questions about whether Ralph had the strong leadership qualities that could inspire us and hold us together as Martin had. Personally, I hadn't felt that Ralph should write his letter to the community while in jail. It seemed to me as if he was copying Martin, trying to emulate him, rather than being himself. Ralph had many gifts, but these gifts were different from those that Martin had. I was concerned that Ralph wasn't using the gifts that God had given him, the gifts that many of us liked and admired. I had begun to see this change during the Poor People's Campaign. Ralph's personality was more folksy and down to earth than Martin's had been. Ralph spoke the language of everyday folks, but he began to play to a different audience. You could see it in his speeches. With Martin gone, Ralph felt that he had to be both himself and Martin.

As the tentative agreement was being worked out, some staff began to return to their previous assignments. Most of the national office staff left, but Ralph, Andy and Hosea of the executive staff stayed on for another week or so to see how the agreement was being implemented. They decided to leave a small contingent of staff in Charleston, and I was one of the staff selected to remain to monitor the situation. If we needed to go back to the streets, we would be on hand to deal with this, and if necessary, request that additional staff return to Charleston.

I was glad to stay in Charleston a little longer because I had come to like the city very much. Scripture speaks of "a city on a hill." The Holy City does not sit on a hill; it sits on a peninsula. But it is a great city nonetheless. Another reason I liked being in Charleston was because Septima Clark lived there. I loved spending time with her and had tried to visit her at least once a week, more often if I could, while I was there.

Mrs. Clark was an important woman in the black community of Charleston, for she had long served the community as a teacher and an activist. She had dedicated her life to serving others, such as the poor black people on Johns Island that she had taught to read and write so they could hold their heads high with pride. She had been my counselor since we had met at the Penn Center in 1965, and she had counseled Martin Luther King even before that. On our visits we talked about many things. She talked about how honored she had been to accompany Dr. King to Norway when he was awarded the Nobel Peace Prize. She talked about her family, her parents, and the guidance they had given her when she was growing up. One day, as I was listening to her soft voice and looking at her gentle face framed by the graying hair, I thought back to when I was a boy sitting on the front steps of our home looking into the face of my gray-haired grandmother and listening to her tell stories. In some ways Septima Clark had become like a grandmother to me. My own grandmother was gone, but this gentle woman with her loving spirit took time to listen to me and guide me. I will forever be grateful.

Charleston was significant for Ralph. He saw it as a personal victory and proof of his leadership, because Charleston was the first campaign organized and put together with him as head of SCLC. Although he had led the Poor People's Campaign, most people viewed that as carrying out what Dr. King had put together. Charleston was Ralph's "baby." Later that year SCLC held its National Convention in Charleston; it was attended by thousands of people. This convention was a way of thanking the people of Charleston for their support of the strong women who had led the union and for their support of SCLC. SCLC used some of the same churches we had used during the strike to hold our workshops and business meetings. We used the Gaillard Auditorium for performances by national artists and for our banquet dinner, where national awards were presented.

After the strike was settled, most SCLC staff left the city and either returned to their old assignments or began work on new projects. While the hospital strike was winding down and Ralph and Hosea Williams were still in jail, Hosea had come up with the idea of going to Cape Canaveral to protest the launching of the Apollo space flight. He wanted to protest the amount of money being spent on the space program compared to how little was being spent on the poor in this country. Hosea felt that we would get good media coverage by doing this. Ralph agreed that it was a good idea and felt that this would be another opportunity to give him more exposure to the national media.

Terrie Randolph and one or two others went to Florida and began to lay the groundwork for this effort. They worked on all of the logistics, such as arranging accommodations for those of us who would be coming and finding a location where we could stable our mule train. This would be one of the last projects to use the mule train, which we used for the first time at the beginning of the Poor People's Campaign. The call came from the SCLC national office for us to bring a contingent from Charleston to Cape Canaveral. Robert Ford and I brought down two busloads of hospital workers and youths who had played a significant role in the hospital strike. In some ways this was a reward for their hard work during the strike. Robert was the only SCLC staff member who stayed in Charleston and made it his home; he is now a state senator, representing Charleston.

When we arrived in Cape Canaveral, I checked in with Terrie to find out where we were to stay and what arrangements had been made in terms of our meals. We had a day or so for relaxation before we began our rallies and demonstrations in the community leading up to the big day–the launch of the Apollo space flight. That was to be the major event.

The day of the launch we descended upon the space center, with Ralph and Hosea leading the mule train, which consisted of several wagons. Several hundred of us followed behind the mule train. I walked alongside the first mule wagon, driven by Ralph and Hosea. Some of the other staff were in front. We made several turns with the mule train in front of the space center as the spectators, who had gathered to watch the launch of the Apollo flight, looked on. After we had made several passes, we left the mule train and marched to a designated area that had been set aside for us. We arrived about forty-five minutes before the scheduled launch. I had never been to the space center before and was fascinated by what I could see from where we were standing. And although I had watched previous launches on television, when Apollo finally lifted up, it was an awesome sight to witness Americans going into space firsthand.

The image that Hosea had originally hoped for was not the image that went out over national television. What the nation saw was Ralph in total awe as Apollo lifted from the ground and into space. The expression on his face was not one of anger and protest, but one of total amazement. This was an extraordinary achievement on the part of the United States. Ralph and Hosea were the only two men in our group to have served in the military, and they must have had a sense of patriotism and pride. He remarked about what an awesome sight it was. So our story and the plight of the poor got lost in the drama of the moment, and we didn't have the impact that we were hoping to have either on the space program or in the halls of Congress.

After Apollo grew small in the sky and the noise died down, the spectators began to leave. We hooked up our mule train and headed away from the space center. In a couple days we reloaded the buses and headed back towards Charleston. The people that we brought with us had had a good time. The hospital workers had a short vacation and the young people had a new experience. Many of them had never left the city of Charleston before.

For me it was an interesting experience, but I was still a soldier on the battlefield, still working for change. I knew that new challenges lay ahead. As we arrived back in the Holy City, I wondered where the next struggle would be, where the next battlefield would be.

The Native Americans
of Ridgeville

It didn't take long before I was given my next assignment. In October, the SCLC office in Charleston received a visit from Mrs. Victoria DeLee, a black woman from Ridgeville, a small town about thirty-five miles north of Charleston. Mrs. DeLee had been arrested in Ridgeville and had been taken to jail in Charleston; she was released after being placed under a $10,000 bond. But before returning to Ridgeville, she decided to stop by the Brooks Motel to ask SCLC for help. Andy Young talked with the woman and then got Ralph, who had returned to Atlanta, on the phone to talk with her as well. Mrs. DeLee explained to them what had been happening in Ridgeville.

Ridgeville had problems relating to the desegregation of the schools. Although blacks had recently been admitted to the public school, a small group of Native Americans, who identified themselves as members of the Cherokee nation, had been denied access. For many years the Cherokees had been attempting to have their children attend the main public school, but in spite of the desegregation laws, they had been unsuccessful. When the Cherokees first raised the issue in 1963, the white community's response was to build a three-room elementary school in Four Holes, the small community outside of town where the Cherokees lived. No provision was made for providing a high school education for the older children. The school that the town built was totally inadequate for the 125 children in the community, and the Cherokees continued to try to get them into a better school.

In 1966 they approached the town once again, requesting that their children be transferred from Four Holes to Ridgeville. Once again, the school board denied their request. The reason given was overcrowding at the Ridgeville School. But during the second half of the 1966/67 school year, the board announced that they would admit twelve of the Indian children into the Ridgeville school. However, before the parents had an opportunity to celebrate this small success, the school board abruptly changed its mind and without any explanation transferred the twelve children back to the Four Holes school. The following year the town provided a trailer to be used as a portable classroom to supplement the space at the small school. The Cherokees speculated that the school board had reversed itself because of pressure from the white community. The next year they appealed once again for their children to be transferred, and once again this request was denied "because of overcrowding."

The Cherokees became frustrated that every request they made in their attempt to get their children a better education was being denied. They turned to the black community for help, since the black community had recently experienced similar problems. When the Cherokees asked them for assistance for the 1968/69 school year, the two communities came together to discuss what to do.

Because the Civil Rights Act of 1964 "forbids racial discrimination in any activity or program that receives financial support from the Federal Government," any school that wished to continue receiving federal support cannot discriminate. Two options were offered by the Federal Government: the Freedom of Choice plan and the Geographic Attendance Zone plan. Under the Freedom of Choice plan, once a year students were given the opportunity to choose the school they wished to attend. This was the most widely used plan, and it was the plan used in the town of Ridgeville.

The two communities made a decision. The black community would not fill out their freedom of choice forms until after the Cherokees had submitted their forms. Both the black and the Cherokee communities suspected that the Cherokees were being discriminated against and that overcrowding was not the real reason why the board was not admitting the Cherokee children. If the black community allowed the Cherokees to submit their forms first, that question would be answered once and for all. Since the freedom of choice process was based on a first come, first admitted policy, then the Cherokees should be admitted. If the issue of overcrowding was truly the reason, then some blacks would not be admitted.

Two weeks before the school was to open for the school year, the Cherokee parents received letters saying that their children would have to remain at Four Holes because of overcrowding at the Ridgeville school. A week later, the black parents were notified that their children had been accepted. So the question for these communities had been answered. The black community decided that if white and black children were able to attend the Ridgeville school, but Cherokee children were not, then they would support the Cherokee community in their efforts to get their children into the school. It was time for new tactics.

On the opening day of school, the Cherokee parents and the black parents took their children together to the Ridgeville school. The Cherokee children and their parents were asked to go to the gymnasium, while the white and black children were instructed to go into the building where classes would be held. A few minutes later, the superintendent appeared in the gymnasium and told the Cherokees that the school was overcrowded and they should return their children to the Four Holes school. The following morning the Cherokee parents took their children back to the Ridgeville school, but once again they were not admitted.

Mrs. DeLee went to U.S. District Court Judge Robert Hemphill and argued that the school board was violating an order that he had handed down in accordance with the Civil Rights Act of 1964. Based upon Mrs. DeLee's report, a hearing was scheduled for September 4, 1968, in Columbia. Judge Hemphill heard arguments from both sides—the school board and the parents. The school board maintained its position that the school was overcrowded, but said that they would admit twelve Cherokee students. The parents argued that their rights had been violated concerning the Freedom of Choice forms. They also argued that the Four Holes school was inadequate. Judge Hemphill ordered that the Ridgeville school must admit fifteen students immediately, and the remainder of the children should return to Four Holes until the next year, at which time the Four Holes school would have to close. The Judge also stated in his order that there should be no interference with the operation of these schools. He further stated that any person violating his order would be charged with contempt of court.

The Cherokee parents felt that the ruling was unfair and that there was a lack of sensitivity to their plight. They felt that they could not in good conscience abide by the order that their children remain in the Four Holes school and decided that they would put all their efforts into getting their children into a better school. The community called a boycott of the Four Holes school. They also called a boycott of the white businesses in the area to put pressure on the school board, hoping to have a little more leverage in the negotiations. For a week, they daily picketed the white businesses. Then the Cherokee parents and the black parents called a meeting with the merchants and asked them to talk with the school board. The merchants met with the school board, and as a result the board voted three to two to admit all of the Cherokee students. These students were enrolled on a Friday, given a list of books, and were told to come to school on the following Tuesday.

But over the weekend, the situation changed dramatically. The white community became angry over the all-white school board's decision to admit the students, and they demanded the resignation of the three school board members who were sympathetic to the Cherokees. The board members were forced to resign and were replaced by three new members. A new vote was taken, rescinding the earlier decision. On Tuesday, the Cherokee and black parents, along with a few white parents who had begun supporting them, went to the school to have the children admitted. Immediately upon arrival at the school, some parents were arrested and taken to the county jail, and their children placed under the care of the Welfare Department. The parents were charged with interference of the operation of the school.

The Cherokee parents who had been arrested began to be afraid to go near the school because they feared that they would be arrested again and sentenced to thirty days in jail for violating the court order. They decided to shift their tactics. For several weeks they drove by the school and demonstrated at the courthouse, which served as the headquarters for the School Department. Then on October 20, while driving by the school, Mrs. DeLee was arrested for being in violation of the court order handed down in September. She was taken to Charleston and placed under a $10,000 bond with a hearing scheduled for early November.

After Mrs. DeLee had explained the situation in Ridgeville to him, Ralph agreed that it was an issue that was right for SCLC. He told her that SCLC would support their efforts but he wasn't sure how long they could stay in Ridgeville. He asked Andy Young to assign staff to the project. Andy assigned me to be the project director and informed Mrs. DeLee that he would assign two more staff members to work with me, but that he might have to pull them out if other situations arose where staff were urgently needed.

I had been a staff member for SCLC for four years by this time. I had served as project director in Greensboro, Troy, and Pickens County, Alabama, and I had first-hand experience with school desegregation in Perry County, Alabama. I had a great deal of experience in direct action and was fairly skilled at organizing and mobilizing people. Andy assigned James Orange and Allan Smith to work with me, and a couple days later I drove to Ridgeville with them to assess the situation. I had worked with James Orange during most of my time in the Movement, but I hadn't known Allan Smith until the Charleston project. Allan was a light-skinned, slim man, a few years older than me. He had been involved with the labor movement and was on loan to SCLC from a labor union. He knew about organizing and pulling people together, but he didn't have the experience with direct action that James and I did.

Ridgeville was very small with railroad tracks running right through the middle of town. On one side of the tracks was a small business district and on the other were the Ridgeville school and other municipal facilities. The railroad tracks not only divided the town, but for the most part they divided the black community from the white community. We drove by the school to assess the environment around it and determine what kind of demonstrations we might be able to conduct, given that there was a federal court order that there should be no interference with the operation of the school. SCLC was cautious about violating federal court orders, although we had done this occasionally in the past. One of the reasons for caution was that we relied upon the federal courts to help protect the rights of civil rights workers, and the rights of black people in general.

I also wanted to get a sense of the Native American community—where they lived, how they lived, and their customs. While at Resurrection City, I had worked with Native Americans, mostly from Oklahoma tribes, and had learned something of their culture and traditions. Because of that experience, I felt that I had gained an appreciation of the ways of different tribes that hopefully would help me establish a relationship with the Cherokees.

The Cherokees lived in a section of town known as Four Holes, an isolated section of Ridgeville. As we left town and traveled down the road beside the railroad tracks, we finally came to the turn-off for Four Holes. The Cherokee enclave was fifty to seventy acres in size and was surrounded by woods. A main road went through the community with a number of dirt roads running off it. Homes were situated on the main road and on the dirt roads. A few families had decent homes, but most lived in trailers. There were no other houses or small grocery stores within two or three miles of Four Holes. This was a completely isolated community, separate from the larger community.

The Cherokees had no formal organization or leadership. There was no tribal council or chief, although several families were active and provided some leadership. One of the reasons for this was that the history and customs had not been passed along. As older members of the community passed away, their oral tradition began to break down, and the younger people did not keep the tradition alive. Another factor was that the Cherokees began to mix with other tribes or even non-Native American people, so that their culture and traditions began to vanish. They began to try to assimilate as other indigenous groups have tried to do over time. Few people in the community had any formal education, and few family members had jobs. A few people had lived outside of the community for awhile and had returned, bringing skills such as nursing that would help the community.

Because of their circumstances, the people did not have many dreams for the future. The young people, in particular, couldn't see beyond their surroundings. They couldn't see a life for themselves outside of Dorchester County. They couldn't see anything beyond family. I believe that this was one of the reasons that they tended to marry and have children at fifteen or sixteen, which perpetuated the cycle of poverty they were trapped in.

I inspected the school that their children were being forced to attend, although by then the Cherokees were boycotting the Four Holes school. After going through the community, I had a meeting with the Cherokee leaders and the black leaders to talk about what to do next and what kinds of support we would need to continue the campaign. After the meeting,

I sent James and Allan to other parts of the county, asking them to make contact with other black leaders outside of Ridgeville. I also asked them to go to St. George, the Dorchester County seat, to look at the jails and get an idea of how many people could fit into them. If we decided to renew our demonstrations, I needed to know how many people we could allow to be arrested at one time. I also wanted the black leaders, particularly in St. George, to know that we would need their support, both in terms of meeting space and logistics support.

One of my biggest concerns was what to do with all the young people who were out of school and receiving no education at all. How could we support these children who were the main focus of this campaign? Ever since the Cherokee community had begun its boycott of the Four Holes school, the children had just been hanging around. They didn't even have recreation facilities where they could spend some time. I was also greatly concerned about the poverty that I was seeing in this community. In addition to the educational issues which we had been asked to assist with, I felt that we needed to look at the community as a whole in terms of the best way we could support them.

Even if I was able to keep James and Allan in Ridgeville with me for most of the time, I knew that the three of us could not do all that needed to be done. Also, our assignment was to be for only a short period of time since SCLC had spent a great deal of its resources while in Charleston. Although at this stage I wasn't sure what I would need from SCLC, I began to identify where we might get some outside resources. One of the first places that I thought of was the University of South Carolina. Although I didn't know anything about the university, I hoped that we might get some support in one form or another from them.

I went to Columbia to see if I could make some contacts. In particular, I was looking for students and professors who might be able to help us, perhaps providing some form of education for the children. I talked to one or two professors in the Education Department about the situation in the Cherokee community. I gathered a few names and asked if I could come back to campus to share what was taking place in Ridgeville. They agreed to provide me with a space where I could speak to a larger segment of the university community.

The following week I returned to the university with Mrs. DeLee and two of the Cherokee leaders, Mrs. Davis and Mrs. Creel. About seventy students and a few professors attended the meeting. Most of those at the meeting were white. The university was going through its own desegregation process, so there were few, if any, black students at USC at the time. I introduced the women and let them tell the story. After they had finished, I told the audience that we were hoping to set up a freedom school. This was something I had done in other communities when SCLC called for a boycott of schools. Depending on the needs of the children, these schools were to provide some form of education, but also to teach them about their culture and history, and how government functions, especially as it related to whatever issues the community was dealing with.

I asked the USC students if they would be willing to come to Ridgeville to support our efforts in a general way, but also described how we would like to have students who would be willing to teach, either full or part-time. After the meeting, a number of students came forward and said that they would like to help. I got contact information for those students who would support our effort for a few hours, as well as for those students who were willing to come and teach, either for a few days or for a longer period of time. I also explained to them that we would most likely be intensifying the demonstrations that had taken place before my arrival.

I left the meeting feeling pretty good. We had made some contacts and were going to get some support. The next big task for me was to find a facility that could serve as a school. We began knocking on doors both in the Cherokee community and in the black communities closest to Four Holes, to see if anyone could help with this. We had no luck until one evening at a meeting Mrs. Davis volunteered the use of a house that her family owned. Members of the family living in the house had agreed to move in with other family members so that we could use the space for the freedom school. The house was one of the largest structures in the community and would provide us with sufficient space to conduct a number of classes at the same time.

The Cherokee families made a commitment to support the school—most importantly, by making sure their children would attend. But the entire community sacrificed to help us. People donated mattresses so that some of the USC students could stay in the back of the school. Other families allowed students to live in their homes. Although they had very little themselves, people cooked for us or brought us food. During the time that we boycotted the businesses in Ridgeville, shopping had to be done in nearby towns, and people would go there to get things for us. This was the first time that the Cherokees had allowed people from the outside into their community, but they welcomed us with open arms and open hearts.

The plan was for the freedom school to operate Monday through Friday, from 9 a.m. to 2 p.m. The primary courses taught would be math, reading, history, spelling, and social studies. But I also wanted the children to learn more about their own heritage and culture. Initially, the students from the University of South Carolina came on weekends to do basic tutoring. This went on for several weeks before we realized that we needed to do something greater if we were going to have a positive impact on the lives of these children whose primary goal was to get married. Two of the USC students, Jack Malloy and his wife, came to me one weekend and told me that they had decided to take a leave from the university, because they felt they could do more to help the Cherokee community if they were in Ridgeville full-time. Other students soon followed their lead. This was good news for me because up until that point James, Allan and I were trying to take up the slack during the week. Most of the USC students went to Columbia on weekends where they lived in dorms or had apartments off campus. During the week I was living in Mrs. DeLee's home. But on weekends I usually went back to Charleston since I still had a room there.

Once we set up the freedom school, we had to figure out how to get the necessary supplies. Some of the students from the university planned to bring materials, but that wouldn't be enough if we were going to do the job that I was hoping to do. I decided that we had to widen our call for support and go outside of South Carolina. We would need more than what I could get from SCLC to support the project.

At the same time that we were searching for outside resources, I decided we needed to put pressure on the white community by resuming our demonstrations and protests. Also, we needed media attention. Once we renewed our demonstrations, I hoped to get some coverage from the Charleston and Columbia TV stations. I called Andy Young and told him what we were planning to do and the reasons for it. I felt we wouldn't be successful in what we were trying to do in Ridgeville without renewing the protests. I added that we would most likely have to violate the court order, although I would be careful about doing that. A few days later he got back to me and said that Ralph had given the okay, but they were going to remove one of the staff members, because they did not want the possibility of all three staff members being in jail at the same time.

At this point I began to widen my network. I began to contact people that I knew or had met in the past. One of the first calls that I made was to Leon Gutherz, the man who had set me on this journey and who had helped me out in Resurrection City. I explained to him what I was doing and asked if he could arrange some speaking opportunities for me in the New Rochelle/Westchester area so that I could try to raise some money and perhaps get some supplies. Leon agreed and arranged for me to speak in Westchester County at four separate events. Another person that I contacted was Joan Madison in Patterson, New Jersey. She and her roommate arranged for me to speak at their church. Also, I contacted the National Council of Churches, and they agreed to send money to support the project through SCLC's national office, designating that the money was to be used for this effort.

But the trip to New York and New Jersey resulted in more than just raising some money and getting a few supplies. I also got more volunteers who agreed to come to Ridgeville. Leon came, bringing a truckload of supplies. Once he had returned to New Rochelle, then his wife Helene made the trip. This was very helpful to us because Helene was an education specialist, with a doctorate in education. In addition to teaching at the freedom school, she gave us great guidance. They didn't make just one trip; they made several. Once again, they showed their support for me and by extension, others. This was the first time that Helene had been down South, other than vacationing in Florida. It was important to me that she was there and that we were working together again. I knew that I could rely upon her, not only because she cared for me, but because she was passionate about education and would guide our young freedom teachers. When she returned to New York, Helene recruited her friends to help us with money and supplies. As I worked with her, I reflected on the first time I had met her that late night in New York City and how she had welcomed me into her home. I reflected on how important she and Leon were to me and how thankful I was that they were in my life.

Joan also made a trip down to Ridgeville to bring supplies. She worked in the medical field and when she saw that the children were malnourished and had other health problems, she realized they needed medical support as well as educational assistance. After she went back to New Jersey, she recruited nurses, doctors, and other volunteers from her church and two other churches. She and her volunteers came down, bringing medical supplies and a medical vehicle where the doctors and nurses examined patients and performed lab tests. They came down more than once, each time staying for a couple weeks. The University of South Carolina had also begun providing medical and dental help for the community, which they continued for a period of time even after we left. In the short time we had been there, not only did we have the educational materials that we needed, but we had gotten other support for the community as well.

Nothing in their past had prepared the Cherokees for all of this. They were surprised and thankful for the outpouring of support they were receiving from people they did not even know.

Another problem for the Cherokee community was that the Federal Government did not recognize them as a tribe and so they were not receiving the kind of support that recognized tribes normally received from the Federal Government. Also, there was little acknowledgment of them by the local and state governments. Although almost the entire community would have been eligible for welfare and food stamps, very few in the Cherokee community received this assistance. Most of the people who worked in the Welfare Department were white and had little regard for the plight of Native Americans. When they went to the Welfare Department, they were humiliated. The Cherokees may have been poor, but they did have pride and were unwilling to suffer this kind of disrespect. So, they went without.

Although the Federal Government did not recognize the Cherokees in Ridgeville, we decided to seek support for them from the Bureau of Indian Affairs. I contacted the bureau, and we made plans to go to Washington, D.C., to speak with the head of the Bureau of Indian Affairs. I felt that if the bureau supported this community, it would give us more leverage with state agencies. Five people made the journey to Washington, but the trip was not as successful as we had hoped. We got very little, in fact, from the Bureau of Indian Affairs. But they did not want us to leave empty-handed, so they offered to provide funds to repay any money borrowed for bail. It was not unusual for the bureau to reimburse tribes for court costs they incurred. Later, when we did have to borrow money for bail, we received some reimbursement, but not all, from the bureau.

I kept reaching out to widen the support base. The people in New Jersey and New York also widened their network and recruited more people. Even the University of South Carolina extended its support by allowing staff to come to assist, in addition to the students we had already recruited. Because of the support coming in to the community, the Cherokees were now willing to risk more and sacrifice more themselves. They were willing once again to return to the streets to demonstrate.

I notified SCLC that we were about to begin the demonstrations again. I called Tom Offenburger, Public Relations Director for SCLC, and told him that I had been trying to get more media coverage and asked if he could assist us in this effort. He agreed to help, so I began to send him audiotapes from our mass meetings and interviews that I conducted with local people. In turn, he and his staff got them out to radio stations.

We began our demonstrations by driving past the school at the time that students were arriving in the morning. I felt that we would be in less danger of violating the federal court order if we were driving on a public highway and were not on school grounds. At least ten cars in a caravan would drive back and forth on the roads near the school three or four times each morning, and then we would leave. We rotated the drivers since the drivers wouldn't be as easily identified if they didn't drive each day. Then we re-instituted our boycott of businesses and began picketing in front of them each day from noon until about 3 p.m. Since the businesses were not close to the school, we were not directly interfering with the school and were not in violation of the court order. But we never knew how the local police and the sheriff might respond to our actions; they might try to stop us from picketing. It was possible that driving by the school could be considered a violation since we knew that Mrs. DeLee had in fact been arrested for just that reason.

We continued in this fashion for several weeks, but finally I decided that we needed to take a more direct approach. In addition to driving by the school, we began marching on the school, although we did not go onto the school grounds. I knew that eventually the authorities would try to stop us from reaching the school, so I did not let the students who were teaching full-time march with us. I didn't want them to get arrested, because it was more important that they be on hand to teach the children. Instead, they watched from the sidelines.

And sure enough, after about the third or fourth march on the school, the sheriff's deputies began to meet us and order us to return to Four Holes. The first few times we would stop and I would either let the sheriff know why we were marching or I would kneel and pray. If we kneeled and prayed, the sheriff would let us pray for a few minutes before ordering us to disband and return to Four Holes. Then, having made our point, we would turn around and leave.

However, as this went on, it became clear that they were meeting us farther and farther from the school and were trying to confine us to Four Holes. I knew it was time for some of us to make the point that we would not stay in Four Holes even if it meant going to jail. I asked Allan to lead a demonstration of about twenty people, to refuse to disperse when ordered, and to continue to march as far as they could. When they had to stop, they should just kneel and be arrested. The night before, we found twenty volunteers who were willing to be arrested. The volunteers were told what to expect and shown what to do. When arrested the next day, they were taken to St. George and bond was posted. A couple of times after that, Allan would gather a group of three Cherokee mothers, two black mothers, and six children and go through this same process until they were arrested.

We continued this pattern for a while and began to gain more attention. More volunteers were coming to Ridgeville to support us. We had been picketing downtown businesses, picketing across from the school, and driving past the school. But we still weren't getting the attention that I thought we needed, so I decided that we must intensify our effort. It seemed to be time to resort to civil disobedience by violating local ordinances. Instead of marching on the sidewalk or on the side of the road, I decided that we would march in the road. We made the decision that a larger group of about a hundred marchers would march this time and I would lead them. We expected to be arrested, and decided that we would refuse to leave jail. Fortunately for us, on the day that I led the march, NBC News was there and recorded us being arrested. I had the opportunity to say to the nation why we were there and why we were willing to go to jail, and this appeared on the Huntley-Brinkley nightly news report that evening. After we were arrested, we went to court, refused to pay bond, and were returned to jail.

I had prepared the people who marched with me, so they were aware that we intended to stay in jail. I had spoken at a rally at a church in St.

George a couple nights before to let the black community there know what we were planning and to demonstrate that we had county-wide support. While we were in jail, people would come and sing outside the jail, keeping our morale up and letting people know we were in there. One of the reasons for refusing to pay bail was to put pressure, not only on the town of Ridgeville, but on Dorchester County and the state. I wanted them all to take notice and be inconvenienced. Since we refused to pay bail, we were filling the jails. If the jails were filled with marchers, there would be no room for criminals. There really was no other place for the criminals to go, therefore the authorities would have to move some of us. If more of us were arrested, Dorchester County might have to use jails in another county.

Another issue that related to our refusal to leave jail was that the county might turn the case over to the federal court, which was fine by me. Many of our victories during the Movement came through the federal courts. I thought we might even be able to bring out some other issues if we were in federal court. We could argue that the school system was not really trying to solve the problem and was using the Freedom of Choice Plan in a negative way. Children who were supposed to be educated in school were now in jail, instead of school. At this point I had the national media on our side, and the officials knew that it was likely there would be more stories. I used this to our advantage.

Most jails were the same physically. What mattered was whether you were alone or with a large group. With a large group you could keep your spirits up by talking, telling stories, or singing freedom songs–songs like "Keep your eyes on the prize, hold on…" and "Ain't gonna let nobody turn me round'…" And that was what we did in the St. George jail. This would be the last of about twenty times that I had been arrested during my years in the Movement. While sitting in the St. George jail, looking out over the square, I reflected on the other times. Most of the times no one was waiting for me and I would just go back to work on the project I had been working on or transfer to another project. Only once–in Greensboro–did I have someone waiting for me.

Ridgeville was under pressure. The media coverage and the growing number of volunteers had the desired effect. But even more important, the Justice Department and the federal courts were applying pressure. Finally, the school board was ready to negotiate an agreement so that our demonstrations and boycotts would be called off. The charges were dropped, and we all left jail. A settlement was negotiated between the parents and the school board for the children to be accepted during the current school year, rather than the following September, when the federal judge had ordered the Four Holes school closed. The federal court accepted the agreement. Although the children would be going to the public school, we decided to keep the freedom school operating so that we could continue to tutor the children and also provide basic skills training to the adults. The students from USC were willing to come to Ridgeville and continue this effort.

In all communities that SCLC was invited into, we tried to leave leaders from the community behind. We trained people to stand on their own and speak on behalf of their community. And this was true in Ridgeville. I felt that it was a part of my responsibility to identify and train leaders from the Native American community. Two women who seemed to have leadership qualities were Mrs. Davis and Mrs. Creel, the women who had accompanied Mrs. DeLee and me to the university to recruit students for the freedom school. Although Mrs. Davis was quiet, I saw that she had a fire within her that only needed to be ignited. Mrs. Creel was more outgoing and was one of the first to go to jail, once we had decided on that tactic. She had urged others to overcome their fears and fight. At every opportunity we had made sure that Mrs. Creel and Mrs. Davis were out front, speaking for their people, talking about their plight and what their needs were.

Unfortunately, Mrs. DeLee felt threatened by our efforts to put Cherokee leaders in the forefront. She was a dominant force in the black community. She had convinced people to support the Cherokees, and was the one who had gotten SCLC involved. In some ways she felt that she was the true leader of the combined black/Cherokee community. When Mrs. Creel and Mrs. Davis began to speak on their own, Mrs. DeLee felt that she was losing her power. She wanted me to consult with her about everything we did. When I told her that I didn't have the time to do this, she became upset and told me that she would like the SCLC staff to leave Ridgeville. Although I respected her, my job was to get the children into the Ridgeville school with their heads held high. I called Andy and Hosea and told them that if Mrs. DeLee requested of them that we leave, I personally would not until I finished the job I was asked to do. I felt that my first loyalty was to SCLC and to the Cherokee community. James and Allan agreed with me. We were united in what we were doing to help change the lives of these people.

I had been living with the DeLee family, so when this situation came up, I was obviously in an awkward position. I moved out of Mrs. DeLee's home and into the home of an elderly Cherokee couple who ran the only little store in that community. When Mrs. DeLee saw that we were not going to back down, she dropped her objections. The conflict ended fairly soon, and we maintained our good relationship with the black community. Over the years Mrs. DeLee continued to be an outstanding leader in Ridgeville. She passed away in June 2010, but a few months before she died, I had the opportunity to be in touch with her. She was still out there fighting the good fight.

About three weeks after the children were admitted to the Ridgeville school, SCLC reassigned me back to Charleston. They did this so that I would be in close proximity to Ridgeville in case I was needed, but at the same time I could be working on voter registration and monitoring the progress of the hospital workers in Charleston. Ridgeville in some ways would be the last major project for me. Ridgeville had been a success. It was a project that I had personally led, a project that I was proud of. I knew when I left that we had set them on a path—a path to reclaim their dignity as citizens. We had set them on the road to being a people capable of speaking for themselves. They would no longer be alone in their struggle, because what we had done there had let the outside world know of their existence. We left them as a community with self-respect and a new voice.

Today the community is officially considered a reservation, and they are known as the Edisto Natchez-Kusso Tribe. The road to sovereignty is a long process. They received recognition from the state in March 2010, but are still working on federal recognition for the tribe.

Providence

After I had finished my work in South Carolina, first with the hospital workers in Charleston and then with the Native Americans in Ridgeville, I was reassigned back to Providence. Upon my return, one of the first things I did was to check on the progress of the demands that Ralph, local leaders, and I had made to the mayor of Providence and the governor of Rhode Island during the Poor People's Campaign–demands related to the poverty issues that affected many people in the state.

I was pleased to discover that we had been fairly successful. The state had put much more money into education and training programs. It had created the Urban Education Center to provide training to adults who were considering college or other educational opportunities. The center would eventually become part of the community college system in Rhode Island. Rhode Island College had begun a summer program for minority high school juniors and seniors to help prepare them for admittance to colleges. The city was providing more funds for the community action program. It was also supporting agencies, such as the Opportunities Industrialization Center (OIC) which provided training. And finally, the city had changed the name of one of its best schools from the Lippitt Hill Elementary School to the Martin Luther King, Jr. Elementary School.

I decided to move the SCLC office from the Pond Street Baptist Church to one of the main streets running through the black community. The street was formerly known as Prairie Avenue, but in the aftermath of Dr.

King's assassination, it had been renamed Martin Luther King Boulevard. I wanted the SCLC office to be more visible, both to the people who lived in the community and to those passing by. The office was across the street from the Urban League, another historic black civil rights organization.

I continued some of the efforts that I had begun before we went off to Resurrection City, but I also began to think about other goals, such as trying to pull together organizations that focused on poverty issues, such as anti-poverty agencies and welfare rights organizations. Before leaving Resurrection City, we had talked about the possibility of establishing satellite "Resurrection Cities" around the country. We had also discussed establishing Poor People's Embassies where organizations could work together on issues and be housed in the same location. Although I was waiting for Ralph to establish an embassy first in Washington, D.C., I was laying the groundwork for forming one in Rhode Island. Another effort I made was to pull clergy together in a form of "Operation Breadbasket." The idea behind this was to put pressure on business and government to create more jobs and training for blacks.

A new effort that I started was a prison program, with an affiliate organization inside the Adult Correctional Institute (ACI). We worked with prisoners on educational issues and tried to prepare them to re-enter society. Rhode Island College, Rhode Island School of Design, and community volunteers helped with high school equivalency and college prep courses. I arranged for both Hosea Williams and Ralph Abernathy to visit the ACI and speak to the prisoners.

Ralph spoke to several hundred inmates, talking to them about changing their lives and said that they had an opportunity to make a difference in their communities once they were released. He got a good response from the inmates. But as soon as we left the prison, Ralph turned to me, putting his arm around my shoulder and said, "John, you brought me into this place with all of these killers and rapists. I'm so glad to be out of there." I knew from Ralph's comment that prison reform would not be on SCLC's agenda. As many times as Ralph had gone to jail, he was clearly uncomfortable in this situation. Most of the times that he had been in jail, he was with staff and supporters. This was different for him. However, I personally felt that prisons could be an opportunity for SCLC to teach the philosophy of non-violence to inmates and perhaps change their ways and even their lives.

One of the people who worked with me in this effort was Roberta Shine. Roberta was an upper middle-class white woman who lived on the East Side of Providence, the section of the city where the richest and most powerful people lived, and was married, at the time, to a well-known attorney, Allan Shine. Roberta had worked with me on the Poor People's Campaign effort and had held a fundraiser with Ralph Abernathy at her home, with the money raised shared between the national SCLC office and my office. Roberta was supportive of my efforts in general. She was a woman who felt that she had to give back and reach out to those less fortunate.

Roberta and I began to see that there were a number of problems facing the inmates at the Adult Correctional Institute. One problem was that Rhode Island had moved its women prisoners to a facility in Massachusetts. As a mother, Roberta was concerned that these women were separated from their children. We felt that some effort should be made to return the women to Rhode Island, so we began to contact other organizations that worked on prison-related issues to enlist their support. Although the State said that they had no place to house the women, we nevertheless felt that we must fight to have the women returned, and the state should find a facility. Rhode Island had a state hospital not far from the prison that had been closed, and we felt that some of those buildings might be retrofitted for this purpose.

Out of this initial effort of mine on behalf of SCLC, a new organization was formed–the Rhode Island Coalition for Prison Reform. This was an umbrella organization where all of the groups dealing with prison issues could come together. Decisions would be made through the Rhode Island Coalition for Prison Reform, and it would be the primary group to speak on prison issues. One of our first efforts was to seek grants. One of the grants that we received was a small one through the Rhode Island Committee for the Humanities for the purpose of holding a series of mini-conferences around the state. One of the speakers that we had at a conference was Dick Gregory, a well-known comedian, who was very much into the prison issue on a national level at that time. This conference was held at Brown University, as were many of the coalition meetings.

Roberta and I continued to push for reform within the Rhode Island correctional system. In addition to pushing for the return of the Rhode Island women inmates from Massachusetts, another priority was to change the direction the prison system was headed. Along with several others,

Roberta and I met with Governor J. Joseph Garrihy, and asked him to appoint a new Director of Corrections. After several months, Governor Garrihy appointed a new director, Anthony Travisano. Travisano was receptive to our idea of returning the women, and he worked very closely with the coalition to make this happen. He moved the Juvenile Training Center to a new location, near Rhode Island College in Providence. By freeing up their former space, along with some of the space that had been occupied by the closed state hospital, Rhode Island was finally able to bring the women inmates back from Massachusetts. We were very successful with several of our major issues, and were pleased when the Rhode Island Coalition was named one of the best advocate groups on behalf of inmates in the nation.

I was still in demand for speaking engagements, both at colleges and community groups, where I talked about Dr. King's philosophy and theology. I appeared on a number of television and radio programs. I did teach-ins. I worked with a number of community leaders, especially Michael vanLeestan and Cliff Monteiro, the two young black men I had met in Alabama who had been so helpful to me when I came to Providence to organize the Poor People's Campaign. They had a clear understanding of Dr. King and his philosophy of non-violence, so it was easy to work with them in spreading Dr. King's message. They were respected by both the black and white community. I also worked closely with Earl Hunt, the director of the Urban League of Rhode Island at that time, on jobs and job training issues.

The Wiley family was one of the mostly widely known black families in Rhode Island and was respected by all segments of the community, both black and white. They were very supportive of me, both in terms of my SCLC activities, but also supportive of me personally, allowing me to spend time at their home in the midst of their family. William Daniel Wiley was very active in the community. He worked for many years at the post office in Providence as a clerk, but also published a community newspaper, which is how I came to know him. He had requested an interview with me for the newspaper, and I was immediately drawn to him, as many others were. His wife, Olive Thomas Wiley, worked in the community with numerous organizations. She mentored young people and also helped her husband with the newspaper. Mr. and Mrs. Wiley sent six children to college, an amazing feat at that time.

Of the six children, I worked closely with Alton and George Wiley. Alton was an attorney at the time, and later became the first black judge in Rhode Island. George had a Ph.D. degree in chemistry and had taught at Syracuse University. But he was widely known nationally as the founder of the National Welfare Rights organization. It was in his capacity as head of that organization that I first met him at Resurrection City. It is unfortunate that George left us too soon. Just as he was having a major impact on the conscience of the nation with his National Welfare Rights Organization, he was killed at the age of forty-two in a boating accident, a sad loss for those of us who knew and admired his dedication and passion for change. George was a major force in how America looked at poor people. He and the welfare mothers in his organization changed the way the welfare system operates today.

Reginald Jones was another of the local soldiers in the fight for freedom. Reggie was working with the Opportunities Industrialization Center as a community organizer when I met him. He had been trained under Saul Alinsky in Chicago and was working the streets of South Providence to help change people's lives. But a few years earlier, the streets had taken its toll on him. He had lost almost everything through alcohol and life on the streets. But fortunately, someone reached out to him, and he was making his way back to a very productive life. I have enormous respect for how he was able to turn his life around and become a model for black men in Rhode Island—both the number of men that he has helped through AA and through his counseling work. He has been sober for more than forty years. Reggie went on to attend Roger Williams University in Bristol, Rhode Island, where he received both his bachelor's and master's degrees, and he set up a very successful counseling practice with his wife Judith Clarke-Jones. Reggie and I became close friends during the period he was with OIC, and we have maintained that friendship up to the present time. Like Leon and Helene Gutherz, he is someone that I consider more "family" than "friend."

I continued to work on issues relating to poverty, voter registration, and political education. I organized some college students, primarily from Brown University, to go into the community to work with me and to provide support to other organizations dealing with poverty issues, such as the National Welfare Rights Organization, Catholic Inner City, and the Urban League. The idea for this project had come from Charlie Baldwin, the chaplain at Brown University, who continued to support my efforts after working with me during the Poor People's Campaign.

During this time I took several vans of Brown students to Memphis, Tennessee, for SCLC's National Convention. Although a couple of the students were from the South, most had never been down South before. One of the students, Michael Tobey, was from Tennessee and knew the area, so he was a good person to have along with us on this trip. Most of these students had some kind of relationship with the chaplain's office, and some were considering the ministry. One of the students, Laura Geller, went on to become one of the first women rabbis in the United States. She is currently a trustee at Brown University.

Another student was Jobeth Williams from Texas. On several occasions Jobeth and I traveled home together. We would drive to Birmingham, Alabama, where she would catch a plane to Texas. Then we would meet in Birmingham on the way back and drive to Providence together. Jobeth was a theatre major at Brown, and she would go into the community and put on short skits for the young people. Or she would do guerilla theatre on the Mall in downtown Providence as a form of protest against the Vietnam War. Jobeth went on to become an actor. After a few years at the Trinity Repertory Theatre in Providence, she began to act in the soaps on TV where she had a major role in *Somerset*. She appeared in movies such as *The Big Chill*, *Kramer vs. Kramer*, and *Poltergeist*. She has continued to act and direct in movies, television, and theater, and we have maintained our friendship over the years.

As time wore on, there was less and less direction from Ralph and the SCLC national office, so I began to increase my non-SCLC activities. Although most of my activities fit into SCLC's goals, there were some that did not fall into the goals that had been set by Dr. King. One of the decisions that I made was to run for public office. After receiving Ralph's blessing, in 1970 I ran for State Representative in the 3rd District on the East Side of Providence. I ran on the Peace and Freedom Party ticket against Fred Lippitt, a Republican and one of the wealthiest people in Rhode Island. Not only was Fred Lippitt wealthy, but he was also one of the most respected and perhaps beloved people in the State of Rhode Island. Fred was very involved in the community. He supported many local community organizations, both financially and as a board member. He was a trustee and supporter of Brown University and served on the board of directors at Rhode Island Hospital, the major hospital in Providence. He had personally sent numerous black people to college with his own personal funds. So, it was surprising to many in the community when I announced my candidacy to run against Fred Lippitt. But if I hadn't run against him, he would have run unopposed because no one on the Democratic side of the aisle was willing to run against him. I felt that by running against him, I could keep some of the issues important to SCLC before the public. Some of those issues were a guaranteed minimum income, full employment, funding for health centers in Providence, and making a state holiday in honor of Martin Luther King, Jr. Also, I felt that by challenging Fred, I could force him to take a stronger position in the legislature if I lost.

It was a very interesting campaign, just because of who Fred and I were–a young black man running against one of the most liberal politicians in Rhode Island–and we attracted a good deal of media attention because of this. Normally a local State Representative race would get no coverage, but in this instance we did. We had a number of well-attended debates. I eventually lost the race, but *The Providence Journal* wrote that I ran a surprisingly strong campaign against Lippitt. I think it had the desired effect and helped Fred look at issues a little bit differently than he otherwise would have. And I think he gained new respect for the entire black community and me. Fred passed away a few years ago and the entire state, including me, paid its respect for the legacy that he left behind. Even though he is gone, he is still having a major impact on Rhode Island, with his bequests to hospitals, colleges, and community agencies.

After I left SCLC, I became even more involved with politics. SCLC was non-partisan, and Martin had not wanted SCLC to get involved in political campaigns. But once I had left, I felt that trying to get people elected, who would fight for our cause within the system, was an option to what I had been doing. I thought I could still have an impact by working for people like George McGovern, Claiborne Pell, Eugene McCarthy, and Hubert Humphrey who had a voice and influence within the walls of power. Working for politicians of that stature would still be a productive use of my organizing skills. Plus, I was really interested in politics, both nationally and locally, and would soon begin majoring in political science at Rhode Island College.

I worked on the George McGovern presidential campaign in several states, and did advance work for his wife Eleanor who was campaigning for him. In 1972, I became a McGovern delegate to the National Democratic Convention in Miami. I had run on the Rhode Island ballot to become a delegate, and fortunately for me the people of Rhode Island voted for McGovern in the primary and therefore elected me to represent Rhode Island as a delegate. This was the first political convention that I would be involved in as a participant, as opposed to protesting outside, so it was a different experience for me. Most of my adult life had been as a soldier in the Southern Christian Leadership Conference. I had worked to bring about change from the outside, having been denied the opportunity to participate in the political process. This was the first time that I would be working for change on the inside.

Life after SCLC

It was becoming clear to me that the Movement was changing. There was very little direction coming from SCLC. Andy Young had left, and Stoney Cooks had replaced him as executive director. Bernard Lafayette had gone into the academic world. And sadly, Ralph did not seem to have a clear vision about where he wanted to take SCLC. Martin had been gone for a couple years now, and the non-violence movement was in its waning days. The issue of poverty was still important to me, but I was also concerned about the increase of violence in the cities and the breakdown of the black family. I wanted Ralph to take on these issues, particularly the violence being perpetrated upon blacks by other blacks. I felt that these could be good issues for SCLC because of its philosophy of non-violence, and that we could do an effective job in this area. I was convinced that we should talk about the violence and the destruction of black families. But these issues were not high on Ralph's or SCLC's priority list. Ralph made several speeches on this issue, but no programs were created.

Not only was the Movement changing, but support for the Movement was also waning. I could clearly see that SCLC was not raising the kind of money that would sustain its current staff level for the long term. I believe that we spent too much money right after Dr. King died and were not as good stewards as we should have been. While the money spent on the Poor People's Campaign was a worthwhile use of SCLC's funds, there was little oversight of staff expenditures in general.

I was working without direction and it often seemed without a real purpose. Ralph would ask me to go and check on some of the affiliate organizations in the East or make arrangements for speaking engagements or meetings with leaders in communities throughout the East. But this was not the kind of work that I was used to or was comfortable with. I was no longer trying to bring about change in people's lives or trying to bring about change in the system. Rather than working to change the world, I was finding myself idle and increasingly frustrated.

I needed to figure out what I wanted to do with the rest of my life, because it was obvious I couldn't stay with SCLC forever. Even if I stayed with SCLC for a little while longer, I knew that I couldn't stay in Rhode Island. At some point, SCLC would want me to come back down South, because that's where its base was. But I wasn't sure that I wanted to go back. By now I had established myself in Rhode Island and had good relationships with a lot of good people that I had come to know through my work there. More and more people on the SCLC staff were leaving for various reasons. What changes did I want to make? Did I want to further my education and gain new skills that would sustain me in the future? Was it time for me to take off my "freedom suit" for another type of suit? Was it time for me to take off the boots that I wore in the heat of battle, for a more calm and peaceful life? I had been a soldier in the fight for freedom for a long time.

In 1971, I notified Ralph that I wanted to leave SCLC to pursue something new. I didn't know what that was yet, but I knew I needed a change. I began to wind down the SCLC activities and look for something else. I closed the SCLC office in Rhode Island, the only official SCLC office in New England since I had shut down the Boston office soon after the Poor People's Campaign. I took off the "freedom suit" that I had first put on in 1965 and hung it in my closet. I would put it on occasionally, mostly in January to honor Dr. King's birthday, until finally with the passing of time I was no longer able to fit into it.

I had spent a good deal of time at Brown University, working with students, both in the community and on campus. When Charlie Baldwin learned that I had resigned from SCLC, he asked me if I would like to come onto the staff of the chaplain's office, working primarily with black students, but with students in general. So, I went to work in the chaplain's office at Brown. Charlie had persuaded the president of Brown that this would be a good move and that I had the skills needed to help students learn about the community and the world. Brown was recruiting more and more black students, and a number of them were from the South. I provided the students with counseling, planning, worship services, and community activities.

Just before Charlie hired me, he had brought the first woman into the chaplain's office, Beverly Edwards. Beverly and I spent a good deal of time together; we were both new and neither of us was ordained at the time. Fairly soon, Tom Willingham was added to the staff. Tom was a Baptist like myself, although he was a Southern Baptist from North Carolina and was struggling with some of the issues in that denomination. Like me, Tom was fairly young, and he and I hit it off because of our age and Southern upbringing. I have stayed in touch with both Bev and Tom over the years.

This was a time when the "Moonies," members of the Unification Church founded by Sun Myung Moon, were a presence on college campuses and were using high-pressure techniques to recruit new members. This group and others prevalent at the time presented a challenge to the chaplain's office in terms of how to protect students, particularly Jewish students, from their approach and philosophy. In response to this situation but also as a way of better serving students, Charlie decided to expand the chaplain's office to different locations around the campus. My new office was located on what had been the Women's College before the merger between Pembroke College and Brown. My office was on the lower level, fairly close to one of the smaller cafeterias, so I was accessible to students gathering in the cafeteria or leaving the building. Bev Edwards had set up an office at the Women's Center, so she was more accessible to women, both students and staff. She eventually became the director of the Women's Center. Tom Willingham was assigned to the Rhode Island School of Design, which is just down the hill from Brown. At that time, RISD had no chaplaincy, so this was a way to expand service to students on the RISD campus.

The chaplain's office was very ecumenical in the sense that most of the Protestant denominations were represented in the office, along with Catholic priests and a Jewish chaplain. Brown University, some years later, would be one of the first universities to hire a Muslim to be a part of the chaplaincy staff. The chaplain's office staff and budget was fairly large, and soon the university began to request that the denominations contribute more to the salaries of the chaplains. Over time the university began to cut back, although Charlie fought as long as he could to maintain the status quo. Slowly, chaplains began to leave the university, including myself.

I felt that I had begun to lose touch with the world outside of Brown and I wanted to get back to the community. I had been spending almost all of my time at Brown, both at work and socially, which began to make me feel uneasy. I felt that I was cutting myself off from the larger world and that somehow I needed to get back into that world. By this time, my friend Reggie had moved to Newport and was now Assistant Director of the Martin Luther King Center, a non-profit agency. He asked if I would like to work with him there as program director. I eagerly accepted his offer since it was just what I was looking for. It was a good job and it would get me back into the community, working with neighborhood people. I joined Reggie at the King Center, but fairly soon after I arrived, he left to join another agency and I ultimately took his place as assistant director.

While at Brown, I had begun to think about education. Bev Edwards was at Andover Newton Theological School at the time, and I often talked to her about what she was doing, which made me focus on the importance of education in what I wanted to do with my life. I began to work for an undergraduate degree at Rhode Island College in Providence. However, I was still working at the King Center in Newport and had to travel back and forth between Providence and Newport most days in order to attend my classes and work at the same time. I was committed at this point to getting an education, but traveling back and forth was taking a toll on me. I soon took a similar position in a social service agency in Providence, which also meant that I could spend more time with Gloria, a young woman living in Providence that I was seeing. I finally graduated from Rhode Island College in 1982. After graduating, I worked with another social service agency in Providence for a few years.

During this period, I continued to work in support of community groups, and I also had a talk show on WICE, a local radio station, where I interviewed a number of national leaders, such as George McGovern and Ralph Abernathy, as well as local leaders. This opportunity had come up because of a national program that SCLC had produced which was broadcast on several hundred radio stations across the country. After the

SCLC program ended its run, I was asked by WICE if I would like to host and co-produce my own talk show.

In 1989 I was hired as the first recycling coordinator for the City of Providence, where I implemented the city's mandated recycling program. This was an exciting opportunity, but after awhile I began to be bothered by how politics affected the work environment and the effect that this was having on me. Employees were pressured to contribute to the mayor's campaign, as well as to work on it. After witnessing the corruption that was taking place, both in the city and in the state at that time, I began to lose my spiritual core. During my time in the Movement, I had a strong sense of who God was and I felt close to God. But at this stage in my life, that was missing. I had stopped going to church on a regular basis, and I began to feel the need to reconnect in a personal way with God. I still felt that God was continuing to call me towards the ministry, but I was not yet ready to answer His call.

By this time, Gloria and I were married and living in Providence. However, after her parents died, we moved to their home in Foster, a rural town in Rhode Island, and I began commuting to my job in Providence. Within a few months of moving to Foster, two incidents took place that moved me closer to answering God's call. First, a cross was burned in front of our home on a Saturday night. The next morning, shaken by what we had experienced, we sought refuge and comfort at a Baptist church down the road from us. Warmed by the welcome we received, we started going to the church every Sunday, and I began to discuss the possibility of seminary with the pastor and with a member of the church who was a seminarian at Andover Newton Theological School.

The second incident occurred after I became a volunteer firefighter in Foster. In addition to fighting fires, the fire company also responded to automobile accidents. One night an accident occurred on a heavily travelled road in Foster, a road that ran from Connecticut to Providence. I crouched beside a man who lay dying in the middle of the highway. I talked to him and did what I could for him, but because I wasn't trained, I felt unable to give him what he needed spiritually in those moments before he died. It was then that I decided it was time for me to answer God's call and go to seminary.

I began going to Andover Newton part time, while I continued to work in the recycling office. After seven years with the City of Providence,

I finally left in order to go to seminary full-time. It took me five years, but I finally graduated with a Master of Divinity degree in 2000. Even before I graduated from Andover Newton, I began working at Bethany Baptist Church, an American Baptist Church in Pawtucket, Rhode Island. At first, I preached on occasional Sundays and then was hired as their interim pastor. Once I received my degree and had been ordained, Bethany asked me to continue as pastor. I served at Bethany for more than twelve years.

Bethany had a predominantly white congregation. I had come from the tradition of the black church, so this was a good opportunity to serve in a church with other traditions. But it meant that I had to change my style, not only in preaching but also in the pastoral role. In the black tradition, the pastor is a much more dominant figure, while the white church is usually run more by committee. In the white church, women have the opportunity to serve at any level, including as pastor, but Bethany was unique in having a young woman, Kathleen Clement, as the president of the congregation at the time they first contacted me. I am especially grateful to her for her leadership and support, and to the congregation at Bethany for calling me to be their pastor.

I loved being a pastor. Martin and Ralph had taught me what it means to be a good pastor–it's more than just preaching. To be a good pastor, you have to listen to the members of the congregation, hear their stories and love them. Martin and Ralph taught me the importance of the social gospel. A pastor has to get outside the walls of the church and into the community and bring the congregation along with him. One of the reasons that I loved Bethany is because of its ministries. Bethany had a food pantry, a housing program for seniors and for mothers who were head of household, and a very good youth program. I was proud of Bethany's work outside the church walls and frequently reminded them that they were answering Dr. King's call for all people of faith to help change the world.

Settling Down

It was not easy to maintain personal relationships or take care of a family while in the Movement. I had watched Martin and Ralph trying to maintain good and healthy relationships with their families in spite of being away from home so often. Martin was away from home more than 80 percent of the time. While in the Movement, I moved around quite a bit from one assignment to another. I worked in some communities for very short periods of time—sometimes a week—while on other occasions it was longer. For example, after James Meredith was shot, I was in Mississippi for a little over two weeks, but when I was in Hale County, Alabama, I was there for months.

So it was not always easy to meet someone, fall in love and keep a relationship growing. And if you have had your heart broken once, it's not easy to open your heart again to trust another and build a lasting relationship. But when I met Gloria in 1970, I was able to open myself up to her and hoped that I had found someone who would love me and whom, without any hesitation, I could love.

Gloria first laid eyes on me in 1969 when I was arrested in Ridgeville. When I had previously worked in Providence, getting ready for the Poor People's Campaign, I met a number of people there, including David and Barbara Schwartzman, a young couple at Brown University. Barbara and David were having dinner with their friend Gloria Hagberg, a Brown staff member, at their home one evening when the Huntley-Brinkley nightly news came on and reported on what was happening in Ridgeville. I was being interviewed by an NBC reporter as the police stood by, waiting to arrest me as soon as the interview was over. Barbara and David were excited to see that someone they knew was being interviewed on national television. So Gloria "met" me for the first time as I was being arrested on national news. This most unusual way to meet is something we still laugh about today. On my return to Providence after the Ridgeville project, we were more formally introduced. We soon began to date, and she is my wife today.

Gloria was with me when I left the chaplain's office at Brown to get back to working in the community. She was with me when I worked at community social service agencies and she was there for me, helping to type my papers when I decided to work for a bachelor's degree at Rhode Island College. Gloria was with me when I started to question what my role in the community should be. Had I given enough? Had I sacrificed enough? Was it time for me to step aside and let someone younger step forth in the community? One of the issues for many of us who came out of the Movement was when to step aside.

Gloria was with me when Ralph came to our home when he was in town. I spent a long time with him, talking about what was happening with him and SCLC, talking about his family and reflecting on our shared past in SCLC and our shared loss of Martin. Gloria was there for me when Ralph passed away, and I went to Atlanta for his funeral. And she was there when I finally realized that the Movement was gone. That it would never be the same because Ralph was gone and I probably wouldn't see again most of the people I had worked with, people I had trusted and put my life in their hands, as they had trusted their lives with me.

Gloria shared all of these moments with me and supported me through them. One of the most difficult moments that she helped me through was the loss of my sister Mattie Jean, who had been shot in her home. When I received the news of my sister's death, I was upset and angry. Gloria kept me calm and focused by reminding me of the task and possible responsibilities that lay ahead, for my sister had two small children, Vanessa and Ron. My mother was getting older, so there was a question of who would take care of my niece and nephew. Gloria raised the possibility that we might have to step forward. Her willingness to think about opening our home to Ron and Vanessa and taking on that responsibility is just another example of Gloria's caring and love for others. Ultimately, however, my mother decided that she would care for the children.

When I lost my father, Gloria was there to help get me through that difficult time. We had earlier bought a place on Seabrook Island in South Carolina so that my parents could make the drive and visit us. Before my father passed away, he and Patsy were able to visit two or three times at our place on Seabrook Island.

When I decided to go to seminary, Gloria encouraged me to pursue my call, to gain the education and skills that I would need in order to go into the ministry. Gloria eventually encouraged me to leave my job with the City of Providence so that I could take more courses and finish sooner, even though the financial load was going to fall on her. After five years, I finally received my M.Div. degree

Gloria has traveled with me through some of the back roads of Alabama and Georgia, and some of these were dark roads late at night. She never showed any anxiety or apprehension, even when we were stopped either for speeding or were stopped just because of who we are—an interracial couple.

In Rhode Island in the fall of 1991, there was a brutal crime involving the Brendel family (Ernest, Alice, and their eight-year-old daughter Emily), who were murdered in a horrific way, although their bodies were not found for several weeks. Gloria worked with Alice Brendel, a Brown University librarian, before her death. The FBI spent a great deal of time in the library while investigating the case, and Gloria formed a good relationship with the FBI agent. Some months later, this relationship paid off when the cross was burned in front of our home.

This was a shocking experience for Gloria, for she had never experienced this kind of hate and violence in her life. Her experience was different from mine, since I grew up witnessing acts of intimidation like this. I had seen the light burning through the darkness of night as the Klan rode the back roads of my home town. This kind of act unfortunately had been somewhat of a routine occurrence in Alabama, Mississippi, and Georgia when I was growing up. But this was not the 1960s on the back roads of Alabama. It was the 1990s in Rhode Island, the state established on the principal of freedom and tolerance. But here we were, still having to deal with this kind of hatred.

The community of Foster rallied around us, but the small rural police force was somewhat overwhelmed and not sure what to do about the incident and how seriously to take it. When the FBI agent realized that it was Gloria who was involved, he offered his support. But even more than that, he assured her that he would make sure that we were protected and that the police followed through with this case and treated it as a hate crime, not just a prank.

Church had not been a part of Gloria's adult life. She believed and had faith, but she hadn't been a part of an organized church as her parents had. But the incident with the cross-burning in front of our home caused her to look at the church in a new light. Because the members of the North Foster Baptist Church had been so wonderful to us during this difficult time, Gloria began to attend that church with me on a regular basis. She became involved in some of the ministries of the church, including becoming the church treasurer. These church experiences helped her when I entered seminary and later became the pastor of Bethany Baptist Church. It made the transition to becoming a pastor's wife much easier.

In 2000, Gloria and I decided to adopt two adolescent children, Danielle and Martina, ten and twelve-year-old sisters in the foster care system in Brockton, Massachusetts. Once again, Gloria sacrificed in order to take care of them and give them a decent home, for they had spent most of their young lives in the system, moving from one place to another. Her willingness to sacrifice is amazing. But more importantly, her warm and open heart is what I admire, and I think all who know Gloria feel the same way. She has an ability to make everyone feel comfortable and therefore everyone loves her as I love her. She is one of a kind.

Gloria and I greatly enjoy traveling together. But it is traveling through life with her that has been the best journey that I have embarked upon. For the journey with her has made me a better human being and a more trusting and caring person. Yes, when I was in the Movement, I cared about the people I worked with and I cared about those whom I was fighting for. But Gloria has helped me to open up on a personal level. She has helped me to see the world and all of its splendid beauty. She has helped me to trust and accept everyone as brothers and sisters.

Her love for me has not wavered, and the love that she has given me has allowed me to love her with all of my heart. It has made me understand what true love is. We have journeyed many places together, but what is important to me is that togetherness. We have shared many joys, but we have shared some tears and pain together as well. We are journeying into old age together, loving one another. I can truly say that I love her with all of my heart and no one except Gloria could have loved me more. And every day I thank God for bringing her into my life. Every night I say, "Thank you, God. Thank you, God, for Gloria.

Some Thoughts about SCLC

As I reflect on the state of SCLC today, as well as on the King family, I am saddened to see what has happened, both with the organization and with Dr. King's children. SCLC fell on hard times some time ago. After Joseph Lowery's tenure as president, Martin Luther King III and Ralph Abernathy III were competing to become president of SCLC. Martin, who had been serving as director of the Martin Luther King, Jr. Center for Social Change, ultimately was named to the position, but did not lead SCLC for very long before he was asked to leave. I had hoped that Bernice, who had just turned five years old when her father was assassinated, would be able to revive SCLC. She was the youngest of the King children, and I was hopeful that she would bring new blood into the organization. She was offered the position of president of SCLC in October 2009, but a year later she came to the conclusion that with two groups claiming to be the legitimate board, the organization was too splintered and divided to be effective. She cited "turmoil, chaos, and confusion" in the organization. I was disappointed that she did not have the opportunity to lead SCLC and move this once powerful organization into the future. More recently, Dr. King's nephew, Isaac Newton Farris, Jr., was elected president, but served less than a year before he too left.

But what saddens me even more is the division that exists among the King children, a division centering mostly on Dr. King's legacy and who controls it. After Coretta King passed away in 2006, this division became more public. While Yolanda King, the oldest of the King children, was alive, there was some hope for the family because she was the glue that held them together. But when she passed away in 2007 at the age of fifty-one, no one filled that role. I was deeply saddened when we lost her, because I cared for her and admired what she had done with her life.

Even in the early 1970s, SCLC was losing some of its luster, and many of the old staff were leaving. Some went back to their old lives—in the church, the academic world, or former jobs. Jesse Jackson, who had been suspended by Ralph for not following the procedures that all of us had to follow, formed PUSH (People United to Save Humanity). Stoney Cooks, Kate Jackson, and Tom Offenburger left to follow Andy to Congress, and then to the UN as members of his staff when he became UN Ambassador. James Bevel went to Chicago and into the ministry. Hosea Williams formed his own organization in Atlanta where he fed thousands of people and worked with the poorest of the poor. His organization at this point was more effective than SCLC was in Atlanta, and he got the national exposure that SCLC was no longer getting. Then in 1976 the SCLC Board asked Ralph to leave. Ralph describes that painful moment in his own book, *When the Walls Came Tumbling Down*. Ralph was succeeded by the Rev. Joseph Lowery, who kept SCLC in survival mode for many years.

In my last year or so with SCLC, I spent a fair amount of time with Ralph, traveling with him and making arrangements for all of his activities in the East. We had quite a bit of time to reflect on the years we had worked together—the highs and the lows. I occasionally spent time with James Bevel, who by then was divorced from Diane. We would assess our efforts at SCLC and discuss our personal growth and failures. We talked about staff members who had passed away, like Bernard Lee, Sunshine, and eventually Ralph and Hosea. In one of our last conversations after we both had left SCLC, Bevel shared with me that he had prostate cancer. Although I had heard that Bevel was facing some legal issues, I was unaware of their nature at the time and was shocked when I learned that he had been convicted of a sex-related crime. After the many times he had gone to jail for the cause of freedom, I was deeply saddened to know that he would be going to prison for that kind of crime. James Bevel, a man with such a brilliant mind, died of cancer in 2009 just a few weeks after being released from prison while appealing his conviction.

During the last few years, I had the opportunity to share time with Bernard Lafayette, who had also moved to Rhode Island, where he created the Center for Non-Violence and Peace at the University of Rhode Island. Bernard spoke at my church on several occasions. We often talked about SCLC's changes in leadership, its financial situation, and its lack of staff that could produce anything close to what we had accomplished. In 2011 Bernard became chairman of the board of SCLC. If there is any hope for SCLC, it may be with him. He knows SCLC's history and philosophy, and he may be able to help shepherd the organization into a meaningful role in the future.

I know that times have changed since the 1960s and 1970s–those years that I fought for freedom. I realize that SCLC must change with time as well. But I am saddened that so far it has not been able to make that transition. Even though it might not be able to change the lives of as many people as it did in the 60s and 70s, I wish it were more relevant in the lives of people today. Andy Young said recently that SCLC should have shut down a long time ago. Maybe he is right. Maybe it is past its time. It may be too late for anyone to save it.

When Ralph passed away in 1990, it was a powerful moment for me. As we carried Ralph's body through the city of Atlanta on a mule train, just as we had done for Martin in 1968, it hit me that the Movement was dead. There would be no more Movement because there was no one to keep us together. Without Ralph, we would drift apart and be drawn into our own lives, perhaps never to see each other again. Only Ralph could have pulled us together for a Movement or even for a social occasion. Now, no one could bring us together, not even for a funeral.

When Hosea passed away, we were not together. When Coretta Scott King passed away, we were not together. When Yolanda King, someone I used to carry on my shoulders, passed away, we were not together. When James Orange passed away a short time ago, we were not together. We were not there to say goodbye to all these warriors who had served so valiantly. When Ralph left us, the end was at hand.

As I reflect on my years going to jail more than twenty times, the blood that I shed, the psychological scars that linger, I realize that those were some of the best years of my life. They are years I shall never forget. And I realize that I have had the privilege of playing a role in redeeming the soul of America. I believe that my work with SCLC helped to change minds and hearts. It helped America refocus on its creed–that all men are created equal. We helped people of goodwill lift their voices and stand up for the dignity of black people and poor people. So in this way, we redeemed the soul of America.

Not in Vain

There was a quietness, a stillness, lingering over the country in the mid-1990s to the early 2000s, when it came to social and political change. There had been almost nothing new from SCLC since Ralph had stepped down in 1977. SNCC was gone. The NAACP and the Urban League did their annual reports. Even college campuses were quiet. On college campuses like Brown, Yale, even the University of California at Berkeley, there was hardly any activity that related to social or political change. Almost nothing was taking place anywhere on a national level, and there was very little even on a local or state level. There was almost no one calling us to a higher level, calling us to fight for the common good. Even I was focusing less on social change and more on my studies as I worked on getting my Master's of Divinity degree.

I had begun to wonder about Dr. King's dream for this country. I wondered if the dream that he laid out for us in 1963 would ever become a reality. Instead, the reality for many was more of a nightmare. Rampant violence and a lack of respect for life seemed to have become a way of life in the black community, and the breakdown of the family structure was a major concern. One of Dr. King's last efforts was to eliminate poverty, but poverty seemed to be on the rise, as opposed to declining. More and more children had little or no health coverage. In most cities, the communities and neighborhoods seemed to be deteriorating. What had happened to Martin's dream?

The only person who would have been able to bring the old SCLC staff back together to continue the fight was Ralph, and he was gone now as well. When Ralph died, I knew that the Movement was finished. He was the only one who had the moral authority and the voice to keep the Movement alive. Jesse's voice and influence had begun to dwindle. Andy seemed to have gone in another direction. And Hosea was also gone; he had passed away in 2000. No one was left to give voice to the problems that exist in America today. No one could call the old civil rights coalition back together for a new battle, a new struggle. Would Martin's dream ever be fulfilled?

Then in 2004 a young man by the name of Barack Obama appeared on the scene. He spoke at the Democratic National Convention and made a connection with people. People began to listen to this new voice. I did not hear the speech at the time it was given, but I caught highlights on the news and was, like many, impressed by what I heard. I then began to wonder if this new voice could mobilize the country once again, as Martin and Ralph had those long years ago. I did not follow Obama's career closely after that, so it would be some time before he came back onto my radar. People were talking about him, and I began to pay more attention, particularly when he came to Rhode Island and Massachusetts on behalf of candidates on the state level. The crowds that he was drawing even then made me take notice. Something was happening and I needed to pay more attention to this young man–this new voice.

Barack Obama was only four years old when I began my journey with Dr. King and SCLC in the Civil Rights Movement. Growing up in Hawaii, Obama was a long way from the segregation and the Jim Crow laws that I had experienced in the Deep South of Alabama. He was a long way from not being able to eat and drink at facilities that only whites could frequent. But like me, he was the son of a single mother who struggled to provide for her family. I identified with him.

On February 10, 2007, in Springfield, Illinois, when Obama announced that he was seeking the office of President of the United States, I knew at that moment that Martin's dream wasn't completely dead. The dream still lived. There was still hope. I knew that Martin and Ralph would have supported Obama, because it was for this that they had struggled for so long. But I was disappointed with some of my former colleagues and friends in SCLC who did not embrace this new voice, this young black man. I felt that those of us who had followed Martin and worked with him should support Obama without hesitation, because this was a continuation of Martin's work and his dream and it would only add to Martin's legacy.

I was particularly disappointed with Andy Young for not coming forth and supporting Obama; instead, he was supporting Senator Hillary Clinton. I could not understand why he could not see that Martin's dream was alive through Barack Obama. It shocked me when Andy, whom I respected, loved and had trusted with my life, made the comment that Bill Clinton was blacker than Obama, that he had done more for the black community than Obama. I personally did not feel that Bill Clinton had moved the lives of black people forward that much. In fact, in my mind he cannot compare to Lyndon Johnson, who had truly enhanced the quality of black people's lives with the Civil Rights Act of 1964 and the Voting Rights Act of 1965, just two pieces of legislation enacted during the Johnson presidency that changed the lives of black people.

I will never question Andy's loyalty to the Movement and his support of Martin and Ralph. But, as I thought about it, I realized that Andy also owed a certain amount of loyalty to the Clintons. He had left SCLC to go into the political arena, where he served as congressman from Georgia for three terms and then as United States Ambassador to the United Nations. During this time he had established a political and personal relationship with the Clintons. I hoped that he would come around as the campaign moved forward. And, in fact, once Hillary Clinton lost the Democratic nomination to Obama, Andy did finally come out in support of Obama.

Although I was willing to cut Andy some slack on this issue, I was not willing to do the same for another former SCLC staff member: Jesse Jackson. Jesse was from Chicago as was Obama. He had witnessed Obama's career and rise as a politician in Chicago from the very beginning. Of all former SCLC staff members, Jesse should have been one of Obama's earliest supporters. He was in a position to know Obama's strengths and weaknesses, so he should have been one of the early people to assess Obama's candidacy. He should have been one of the people helping the rest of the nation understand who this young man from Chicago was. He should have been the one reaching out to those of us who had come out of the Movement as he had—those of us who most likely were going to try to register new voters. But I believe that Jesse's ego came into play, as his ego had always come into play. It was more about him than the Obama campaign. Obama was a threat to Jesse and his leadership. That was clearly evident as the campaign went on, and Jesse made several negative remarks about Obama. However, I believe that Jesse's reputation was damaged by these comments and his weak support of Obama.

It was Joseph Lowery, a member of the SCLC Board, and the person who succeeded Ralph as president of SCLC, who came out clearly in support of Obama, and he encouraged the black community to support him. Even John Lewis, who grew up in the same hometown that I did, initially supported Hillary Clinton for president. But this veteran of the Civil Rights Movement soon realized that the wind was blowing in a new direction. He could feel the wind of a new Movement and he finally came out in support of Barack Obama.

The black community itself was slow at first to support Obama, and their hesitation was somewhat of a surprise. But as I reflected on it, I could see why they hesitated. They must have wondered if Dr. King's dream was still alive and whether Obama was the person that Dr. King had spoken about in 1963 when he shared his dream with all of us. They were dealing with their own disappointment and disillusionment, so they couldn't believe, and in fact dared not believe, that it was possible for a black man to become president. But finally, people became galvanized in a way I had never seen before.

We in the Movement had motivated black people to stand up and fight for freedom. But Obama was reaching out beyond the black community. Without early support from the black leadership and the larger black community, Obama forged ahead in his effort to put a coalition together to become president. He was putting together the coalition—the poor whites, the blacks, the browns, and the reds—that Martin tried to put together with the Poor People's Campaign before he was assassinated. Obama had learned from those of us in the old Movement. He had seen what we had produced, how we had taken people to the streets. He had become a community organizer as I had been and had studied under Saul Alinsky. He used all his skills as a community organizer to set up a smoothly run campaign, and set up mechanisms to mobilize people across the country in a way that was similar to what Dr. King had done back in the 60s. He was putting people in the streets, into churches and halls, all across America.

Obama had taken these strategies to a new level, and this coalition was clearly working as had never been seen before.

One of the things that we had been lacking for the last twenty years was someone who could inspire and mobilize a broad section of this country and bring people together. Obama had the gift and ability to inspire people to go beyond themselves. Like Martin, he inspired both the young and the old. Using his organizing background, he mobilized college campuses, teaching young people the techniques of organizing and motivating people to take action. He was able to get people to look, not just within, but to look beyond themselves, beyond their own needs. He was able to get people to sacrifice for something much larger. And that's what Martin did throughout his life—he motivated people to make the necessary sacrifices for social change. That was certainly true for me in my journey with Martin and SCLC. My life was never the same after that, because I will always look beyond myself. Martin made me realize there was something larger and more important than self.

Obama was able to go to a state with a largely white population and mobilize people in a way that had never been done before. He made them believe and he mobilized them. Because he did that, he was able to demonstrate that he could win. He showed the black community that he could win. He showed that the dream was still at hand. He showed that he could bring the country together—that he could unite all of us. For me, it was particularly interesting to see this unfold—to see the skills and the gifts that he had, and his use of those skills.

The Obama campaign had lifted the spirits of so many. For the first time, it seemed possible that a black person might be elected President of the United States. Black people had experienced the campaign of Shirley Chisholm in 1972, the first woman to run for president, but there was a sense that she couldn't make it. They had even experienced the campaign of Jesse Jackson in 1988, but with that same sense that it would not go anywhere. But now, those people that I helped usher into the courthouse in 1965 had a new reality. They had a new hope. They could see Dr. King's dream coming true through Obama. They could feel this new reality. So their spirits were soaring. Those people that I had helped to register to vote were standing tall all over the country. They were willing to stand long hours in the rain and in the heat, in order that their votes might be counted. Before 1965, my mother never dreamed that she would ever have the opportunity to vote. But now she was determined that she was not going to let anything stop her from voting–pain, rain, fear would not stop her this time. Only God could stop her. For me, it was an affirmation of my work and my sacrifice; it all had a purpose.

The fact that Obama was nominated at the Democratic National Convention essentially on the anniversary of the same date that Dr. King had pronounced his dream was very meaningful for me. It was a connection that moved me; it overwhelmed me. At that moment the similarities between Obama and Dr. King became clear to me. They were similar in their education and in the gifts that God had given to both of them. On that night, when the masses came to witness his nomination, it took me back to that young Martin Luther King in his twenties who began to move the people of Montgomery. And now there stood another young man who was moving the masses of this country. In some ways I was even more moved on that August evening than I was on the night of November 4 when he won the election. It was also significant to me that on January 19, 2009 we celebrated the birth of Martin Luther King, and then on the following day, the first black was inaugurated as president. It seemed to me that God had orchestrated this–that He wanted the connection of these two men to be lifted up before the people of the world.

What Obama was able to do during the two-year campaign was extraordinary. He had changed the country, as Martin had changed the country forty years earlier. He had moved people by his intellect, by his commitment to serve, and by his vision and eloquence. So what I was feeling on the night of November 4 was that all of my suffering, the times that I went to jail and was beaten were not in vain.

I thought back to the first time that Leon and I walked into the courthouse in Troy, Alabama, to tell the registrar that we would be bringing people in to register to vote, and I remembered how nervous I was that day. I thought of the first group of people that Leon and I brought into the courthouse, remembering the tension and the fear on their faces. I reflected on the day that my mother walked to the courthouse to register, her face tense and unsmiling, slowly making her way up the line into the courthouse. I remembered those first people who were able to register, the joy in their eyes, the excitement of accomplishing something they had been hoping to do for a long time.

On January 20, 2009, more than two million people stood huddled together peacefully in the bitter cold to witness Barack Obama being sworn in. Across America, millions more witnessed this moment on television. Many more were in theaters and in parks across the country. The world came to a stop because of this man who had inspired so many–to witness Barack Obama becoming President. When I was registering all of those folks in the Deep South, I never imagined that I would witness this moment. But even more important, that my mother would be able to witness this moment–that it would happen in her lifetime. She was more excited about Obama than she ever was about Martin. These millions of people were a witness to the moment that Martin had dreamed of more than forty years before. It was a moment that they never will forget, like the moment for those who were witness to Martin's dream in 1963.

I reflected on all the battles I had endured, all of the sacrifices, all of the times in jail, the shedding of my blood. Obama's election was affirmation for Martin and Ralph and for all of the others, like Rosa Parks, who had put their lives on the line. I reflected on all of those who marched across the Edmund Pettus Bridge on Bloody Sunday. I remembered Martin assisting the elderly black people of Selma into the courthouse himself. I reflected on all of those who had given their lives in order to register poor and black people so that they could put their hand on the lever of a voting machine. It was affirmation for all of them: Viola Liuzzo who gave her life helping the black people of Selma, Alabama, where she was gunned down on a darkened Highway 80 outside of town; the Rev. Jim Reeb, who was beaten to death in downtown Selma for giving support and voice to the black people of Selma; Jonathan Daniels who was shot while protecting a young black girl in Lowndes County; Jimmy Lee Jackson of Marian, Alabama, who gave his life for the people of Marian; and Andrew Goodman, Michael Schwerner, and James Chaney, who gave their lives in Mississippi. Their deaths were not in vain. Not a month goes by that I do not think of them and honor them, for they were true freedom fighters who gave their lives on the battlefield. As I reflected, I knew that Martin's dream was not yet dead. After all of the battles and bloodshed, it was not in vain. All of us, for a little while, those that are here and those that have gone, could celebrate the triumph through the election of Barack Obama.

It saddened me that Martin and Ralph were not there to witness the inauguration, not there to see the fruit of their labor. If they were still with us, they would surely have been in a place of honor at the Capitol on that cold January morning. Joseph Lowery, Ralph's successor as President of SCLC, and one of the earliest black leaders to support Obama, was there and he gave the benediction at the inaugural ceremony.

Forty years before Obama was sworn in as President of the United States, Martin Luther King was assassinated while working on behalf of sanitation workers. As Obama was sworn in, I said to myself, "Martin, the sacrificing of your life was not in vain. Your dream is truly alive in this moment. I thank you for all that you did for me and all that you did for the world."